Lectures on Faith

Restoration Edition

The Complete Original 1835 Text including KJV Citations
Together with Citations to the Restoration Edition of the Scriptures

Paperback ISBN 978-1-951168-70-4
Hardcover ISBN 978-1-951168-69-8

©2020 Restoration Scriptures Foundation
All Rights Reserved

Table of Contents

Explanation of the Restoration Edition..5

Preface..7

LECTURE FIRST...9

LECTURE SECOND...17

LECTURE THIRD..45

LECTURE FOURTH...55

LECTURE FIFTH...63

LECTURE SIXTH...71

LECTURE SEVENTH...75

Appendix: Chronology of the Fathers..85

Explanation of the Restoration Edition

Lectures on Faith restores foundational understanding of faith and spirituality that have been neglected, pushed aside, and forgotten. Its objective is to teach the reader what faith is, the object(s) upon which it rests, and the effects that flow from it.

The visionary Joseph Smith, Jr. personally edited and vouched for the Lectures on Faith in 1834, which were subsequently adopted as Scripture in 1835 during a General Conference of the Church of Jesus Christ of Latter Day Saints by common consent. The Lectures were then published in 1835 as the first major part of Doctrine and Covenants (D&C), comprising the "doctrine" portion of the volume, and rendered in a font larger and more prominent than the "covenants" portion that contained the revelations and instructions that followed.

In 1921, a committee quietly removed the "doctrine" (Lectures on Faith) portion of Doctrine and Covenants. Since then, all major sects have quietly removed them from their body of Scriptures, though not by common consent. It remains canonized Scripture today.

This Restoration Edition of Lectures on Faith was re-published in 2019 by an independent group of volunteers as part of an ongoing effort to recover sacred Scripture, restore it back to the original text as precisely and completely as possible, and preserve it for future generations. This edition restores the text to the original and updates and corrects punctuation to current standards.

Scriptural citations within the text include the original citation used in the 1835 edition, together with citations to the Restoration Edition of the Scriptures, which are notated using brackets, as in [Gen. 3:15].

The complete Restoration Edition of the Scriptures can be found online at:
>http://scriptures.info

Comments can be sent to info@restorationarchives.com.

Preface

A preface to the 1835 Doctrine and Covenants written 17 February 1835, and signed by all four members of the committee who compiled the volume.

To the members of the church of the Latter Day Saints—

Dear Brethren:

We deem it to be unnecessary to entertain you with a lengthy preface to the following volume, but merely to say that it contains, in short, the leading items of the religion which we have professed to believe.

The first part of the book will be found to contain a series of lectures as delivered before a theological class in this place, and in consequence of their embracing the important doctrine of salvation, we have arranged them into the following work.

The second part contains items or principles for the regulation of the church, as taken from the revelations which have been given since its organization, as well as from former ones.

There may be an aversion in the minds of some against receiving anything purporting to be articles of religious faith, in consequence of there being so many now extant; but if men believe a system, and profess that it was given by inspiration, certainly, the more intelligibly they can present it, the better. It does not make a principle untrue to print it, neither does it make it true not to print it.

The church, viewing this subject to be of importance, appointed through their servants and delegates, the high council, your servants to select and compile this work. Several reasons might be adduced in favor of this move of the council, but we only add a few words. They knew that the church was evil spoken of in many places—its faith and belief misrepresented, and the way of truth thus subverted. By some it was represented as disbelieving the Bible, by others as being an enemy to all good order and uprightness, and by others as being injurious to the peace of all governments, civil and political.

We have therefore endeavored to present, though in few words, our belief; and when we say this, humbly trust the faith and principles of this society as a body.

We do not present this little volume with any other expectation than that we are to be called to answer to every principle advanced, in that day when the secrets of all hearts will be revealed, and the reward of every man's labor will be given him.

With sentiments of esteem and sincere respect, we subscribe ourselves your brethren in the bonds of the gospel of our Lord Jesus Christ.

JOSEPH SMITH Jr.
OLIVER COWDERY.
SIDNEY RIGDON.
F. G. WILLIAMS.

                                          Kirtland, Ohio, February 17, 1835.

THEOLOGY

LECTURE FIRST

Of Faith

1. Faith, being the first principle in revealed religion, and the foundation of all righteousness, necessarily claims the first place in a course of lectures which are designed to unfold to the understanding the doctrine of Jesus Christ.

2. In presenting the subject of faith, we shall observe the following order:

3. First, faith itself—what it is,

4. Secondly, the object on which it rests, and

5. Thirdly, the effects which flow from it.

6. Agreeably to this order we have first to show what faith is.

7. The author of the epistle to the Hebrews, in the eleventh chapter of that epistle, and first verse, [Heb. 1:36], gives the following definition of the word faith:

8. Now faith is the substance (assurance) of things hoped for, the evidence of things not seen.

9. From this we learn that faith is the assurance which men have of the existence of things which they have not seen and the principle of action in all intelligent beings.

10. If men were duly to consider themselves, and turn their thoughts and reflections to the operations of their own minds, they would readily discover that it is faith, and faith only, which is the moving cause of all action in them; that without it, both mind and body would be in a state of inactivity and all their exertions would cease, both physical and mental.

11. Were this class to go back and reflect upon the history of their lives, from the period of their first recollection, and ask themselves what principle excited them to action, or what gave them energy and activity in all their lawful avocations, callings, and pursuits, what would be the answer? Would it not be that it was the assurance which we had of the existence of things which we had not seen, as yet? Was it not the hope which you had, in consequence of your belief in the existence of unseen things, which stimulated you to action and exertion in order to obtain them? Are you not dependent on your faith, or belief, for the acquisition of all knowledge, wisdom, and intelligence? Would you exert yourselves to obtain wisdom and intelligence unless you did believe that you could obtain them? Would you have ever sown if you had not believed that you would reap? Would you have ever planted if you had not believed that you would gather? Would you have ever asked unless you had believed that you would receive? Would you have ever sought unless you had believed that you would have found? Or would you have ever knocked unless you had believed that it would have been opened unto you? In a word, is there anything that you would have done, either physical or mental, if you had not previously believed? Are not all your exertions, of every kind, dependent on your faith? Or may we not ask, what have you, or what do you possess, which you have not obtained by reason of your faith? Your food, your raiment, your lodgings, are they not all by reason of your faith? Reflect and ask yourselves if these things are not so. Turn your thoughts on your own minds and see if faith is not the moving cause of all action in yourselves; and if the moving cause in you, is it not in all other intelligent beings?

12. And as faith is the moving cause of all action in temporal concerns, so it is in spiritual; for the Savior has said, and that truly, that he that believeth and is baptized shall be saved (Mark 16:16) [Mark 8:6].

13. As we receive by faith all temporal blessings that we do receive, so we, in like manner, receive by faith all spiritual blessings that we do receive. But faith is not only the principle of action, but of power also, in all intelligent beings, whether in Heaven, or on earth. Thus says the author of the epistle to the Hebrews, 11:3 [Heb. 1:36]:

14. Through faith we understand that the worlds were framed by the word of God, so that things which are seen were not made of things which do appear.

15. By this we understand that the principle of power which existed in the bosom of God, by which the worlds were framed, was faith, and that it is by reason of this principle of power existing in the Deity that all created things exist—so that all things in Heaven, on earth, or under the earth, exist by reason of faith, as it existed in him.

16. Had it not been for the principle of faith, the worlds would never have been framed, neither would man have been formed of the dust—it is the principle by which Jehovah works and through which he exercises power over all temporal, as well as Eternal things. Take this principle or attribute (for it is an attribute) from the Deity and he would cease to exist.

17. Who cannot see that if God framed the worlds by faith, that it is by faith that he exercises power over them and that faith is the principle of power? And that if the principle of power, it must be so in man as well as in the Deity? This is the testimony of all the sacred writers and the lesson which they have been endeavoring to teach to man.

18. The Savior says, Matthew 17:19, 20 [Matt. 9:7], in explaining the reason why the disciples could not cast out the devil, that it was because of their unbelief: For verily, I say unto you, said he, if ye have faith as a grain of mustard seed, ye shall say unto this mountain, Remove hence to yonder place!—and it shall remove; and nothing shall be impossible unto you.

19. Moroni, while abridging and compiling the record of his fathers, has given us the following account of faith as the principle of power: he says, page 563 [Ether 5:3], that it was the faith of Alma and Amulek which caused the walls of the prison to be rent, as recorded on the 264th page [Alma 10:11]; that it was the faith of Nephi and Lehi which caused a change to be wrought upon the hearts of the Lamanites when they were immersed with the holy

spirit and with fire, as seen on the 421st page [Hel. 2:25]; and that it was by faith the mountain Zerin was removed when the brother of Jared spake in the name of the Lord. See also 565th page [Ether 5:6].

20. In addition to this we are told in Hebrews, 11:32,33,34,35 [Heb. 1:49], that Gideon, Barak, Samson, Jephthah, David, Samuel, and the prophets, through faith subdued kingdoms, wrought righteousness, obtained promises, stopped the mouths of lions, quenched the violence of fire, escaped the edge of the sword, out of weakness were made strong, waxed valiant in fight, turned to flight the armies of the aliens, and that women received their dead raised to life again, etc.

21. Also, Joshua, in the sight of all Israel, bade the sun and moon to stand still, and it was done (Joshua 10:12) [Josh. 2:19].

22. We here understand that the sacred writers say that all these things were done by faith. It was by faith that the worlds were framed: God spake, chaos heard, and worlds came into order by reason of the faith there was in him. So with man also: he spake by faith in the name of God and the sun stood still, the moon obeyed, mountains removed, prisons fell, lions' mouths were closed, the human heart lost its enmity, fire its violence, armies their power, the sword its terror, and death its dominion, and all this by reason of the faith which was in him.

23. Had it not been for the faith which was in man, they might have spoken to the sun, the moon, the mountains, prisons, lions, the human heart, fire, armies, the sword, or to death in vain!

24. Faith, then, is the first great governing principle which has power, dominion, and authority over all things: by it they exist, by it they are upheld, by it they are changed, or by it they remain, agreeably to the will of God. Without it there is no power, and without power there could be no creation, nor existence!

Questions and Answers on the Foregoing Principles

25. Question 1: What is theology?

Answer: It is that revealed science which treats of the being and attributes of God, his relations to us, the dispensations of his providence, his will with respect to our actions, and his purposes with respect to our end (Buck's Theological Dictionary, page 582).

26. Question 2: What is the first principle in this revealed science?
A: Faith (¶1).

27. Question 3: Why is faith the first principle in this revealed science?
A: Because it is the foundation of all righteousness. Hebrews 11:6 [Heb. 1;38]: Without faith it is impossible to please God. 1 John 3:7 [1 John 1:14]: Little children, let no man deceive you: he that doeth righteousness is righteous, even as he (God) is righteous (¶1).

28. Question 4: What arrangement should be followed in presenting the subject of faith?
A: First, it should be shown what faith is (¶3);

Secondly, the object upon which it rests (¶4); and

Thirdly, the effects which flow from it (¶5).

29. Question 5: What is faith?
A: It is the assurance of things hoped for, the evidence of things not seen (Hebrews 11:1) [Heb. 1:36]. That is, it is the assurance we have of the existence of unseen things. And being the assurance which we have of the existence of unseen things, must be the principle of action in all intelligent beings. Hebrews 11:3 [Heb. 1:36]: Through faith we understand the worlds were framed by the word of God (¶¶ 8, 9).

30. Question 6: How do you prove that faith is the principle of action in all intelligent beings?
A: First, by duly considering the operations of my own mind, and secondly, by the direct declaration of scripture. Hebrews 11:7 [Heb. 1:39]: By faith Noah, being warned of things not seen as yet, moved with fear, prepared an ark to the saving of his house, by the which he condemned the world and became heir of the righteousness

which is by faith. Hebrews 11:8 [Heb. 1:40]: By faith Abraham, when he was called to go out into a place which he should after receive for an inheritance, obeyed, and he went out not knowing whither he went. Hebrews 11:9 [Heb. 1:40]: By faith he sojourned in the land of promise, as in a strange country, dwelling in tabernacles with Isaac and Jacob, the heirs with him of the same promise. Hebrews 11:27 [Heb. 1:47]: By faith Moses forsook Egypt, not fearing the wrath of the king, for he endured as seeing him who is invisible (¶¶10–11).

31. Question 7: Is not faith the principle of action in spiritual things as well as in temporal?
A: It is.

32. Question 8: How do you prove it?
A: Hebrews 11:6 [Heb. 1:38]: Without faith it is impossible to please God. Mark 16:16 [Mark 8:6]: He that believeth and is baptized shall be saved. Romans 4:16 [Rom. 1:20]: Therefore, it is of faith, that it might be by grace, to the end the promise might be sure to all the seed: not to that only which is of the law, but to that also which is of the faith of Abraham, who is the father of us all (¶¶12–13).

33. Question 9: Is faith anything else besides the principle of action?
A: It is.

34. Question 10: What is it?
A: It is the principle of power also (¶13).

35. Question 11: How do you prove it?
A: First, it is the principle of power in the Deity, as well as in man. Hebrews 11:3 [Heb. 1:36]: Through faith we understand that the worlds were framed by the word of God, so that things which are seen were not made of things which do appear (¶¶14–16).

36. Secondly, it is the principle of power in man also. Book of Mormon, page 264 [Alma 10:11]. Alma and Amulek are delivered from prison. Ditto, page 421 [Hel. 2:24–26]. Nephi and Lehi, with the Lamanites, are immersed with the spirit. Ditto, page 565 [Ether 5:6]. The mountain Zerin, by the faith of the brother of Jared, is

removed. Joshua 10:12 [Joshua 2:19]: Then spake Joshua to the Lord in the day when the Lord delivered up the Amorites before the children of Israel, and he said in the sight of Israel, Sun, stand thou still upon Gibeon, and thou Moon, in the valley of Ajalon. Joshua 10:13 [Joshua 2:19]: And the sun stood still, and the moon stayed, until the people had avenged themselves of their enemies. Is not this written in the book of Jasher? So the sun stood still in the midst of heaven and hasted not to go down about a whole day. Matthew 17:19 [Matt. 9:7]: Then came the disciples to Jesus apart and said, Why could not we cast him out? Matthew 17:20 [Matt 9:7]: And Jesus said unto them, Because of your unbelief: for verily I say unto you, if ye have faith as a grain of mustard seed, ye shall say unto this mountain, Remove hence to yonder place, and it shall remove; and nothing shall be impossible unto you. Hebrews 11:32 [Heb. 1:49]: And what shall I say more? For the time would fail me to tell of Gideon, and of Barak, and of Samson, and of Jephthah, of David also, and Samuel, and of the prophets, Hebrews 11:33 [Heb. 1:49]: who through faith subdued kingdoms, wrought righteousness, obtained promises, stopped the mouths of lions, Hebrews 11:34 [Heb. 1:49]: quenched the violence of fire, escaped the edge of the sword, out of weakness were made strong, waxed valiant in fight, turned to flight the armies of the aliens. Hebrews 11:35 [Heb. 1:49]: Women received their dead raised to life again, and others were tortured, not accepting deliverance; that they might obtain a better resurrection (¶¶16–22).

37. Question 12: How would you define faith in its most unlimited sense?
A: It is the first great governing principle, which has power, dominion, and authority over all things (¶24).

38. Question 13: How do you convey to the understanding more clearly that faith is the first great governing principle, which has power, dominion, and authority over all things?
A: By it they exist, by it they are upheld, by it they are changed, or by it they remain, agreeably to the will of God; and without it there is no power; and without power there could be no creation, nor existence! (¶24).

LECTURE SECOND

Of Faith

1. Having shown in our previous lecture faith itself—what it is, we shall proceed to show secondly the object on which it rests.

2. We here observe that God is the only supreme governor and independent being in whom all fullness and perfection dwells; who is omnipotent, omnipresent, and omniscient, without beginning of days or end of life, and that in him every good gift and every good principle dwells, and that he is the Father of Lights: in him the principle of faith dwells independently; and he is the object in whom the faith of all other rational and accountable beings centers for life and salvation.

3. In order to present this part of the subject in a clear and conspicuous point of light, it is necessary to go back and show the evidences which mankind have had, and the foundation on which these evidences are, or were, based since the creation, to believe in the existence of a God.

4. We do not mean those evidences which are manifested by the works of creation, which we daily behold with our natural eyes: we are sensible that after a revelation of Jesus Christ, the works of creation, throughout their vast forms and varieties, clearly exhibit his eternal power and Godhead. Romans 1:20 [Rom. 1:4]: For the invisible things of him from the creation of the world are clearly seen, being understood by the things that are made: even his eternal power and Godhead. But we mean those evidences by which the first thoughts were suggested to the minds of men that there was a God who created all things.

5. We shall now proceed to examine the situation of man at his first creation. Moses, the historian, has given us the following account of him in the first chapter of the book of Genesis, beginning with the 20th verse, and closing with the 30th [Gen. 2:8–9]. We copy from the New Translation:

6. And the Lord God said unto the Only Begotten, who was with him from the beginning, Let us make man in our image, after our likeness: and it was done.

7. And the Lord God said, Let them have dominion over the fish of the sea, and over the fowl of the air, and over the cattle, and over all the earth, and over every creeping thing that creeps upon the earth.

8. So God created man in his own image, in the image of the Only Begotten created he him: male and female created he them. And God blessed them, and God said unto them, Be fruitful, and multiply, and replenish the earth, and subdue it: and have dominion over the fish of the sea, and over the fowl of the air, and over every living thing that moves upon the earth.

9. And the Lord God said unto man, Behold, I have given you every herb bearing seed, which is upon the face of all the earth, and every tree in the which is the fruit of a tree yielding seed; to you it shall be for meat.

10. Again, Genesis 2:15,16,17,19,20 [Gen. 2:13]: And the Lord God took the man and put him into the Garden of Eden, to dress it and to keep it. And the Lord God commanded the man saying, Of every tree of the garden you may freely eat, but of the tree of the knowledge of good and evil you shall not eat of it, neither shall you touch it; nevertheless, you may choose for yourself, for it is given unto you, but remember that I forbid it, for in the day that you eat thereof you shall surely die.

11. And out of the ground the Lord God formed every beast of the field and every fowl of the air, and commanded that they should be brought unto Adam to see what he would call them. And whatever Adam called every living creature, that was the name thereof. And Adam gave names to all cattle, and to the fowl of the air, and to every beast of the field.

12. From the foregoing we learn man's situation at his first creation: the knowledge with which he was endowed, and the high and exalted station in which he was placed—lord or governor of all

Lecture Second   19

things on earth, and at the same time enjoying communion and intercourse with his Maker without a veil to separate between. We shall next proceed to examine the account given of his fall, and of his being driven out of the Garden of Eden and from the presence of the Lord.

13. Moses proceeds: And they (Adam and Eve) heard the voice of the Lord God as they were walking in the garden in the cool of the day, and Adam and his wife hid themselves from the presence of the Lord God among the trees of the garden. And the Lord God called unto Adam and said unto him, Where are you going? And he said, I heard your voice in the garden, and I was afraid because I beheld that I was naked, and I hid myself.

14. And the Lord God said unto Adam, Who told you that you were naked? Have you eaten of the tree whereof I told you that you should not eat? If so, you should surely die? And the man said, The woman whom you gave me, and commanded that she should remain with me, gave me of the fruit of the tree and I did eat.

15. And the Lord God said unto the woman, What is this which you have done? And the woman said, The serpent beguiled me and I did eat.

16. And again, the Lord said unto the woman, I will greatly multiply your sorrow and your conception: in sorrow you shall bring forth children; and your desire shall be to your husband, and he shall rule over you.

17. And the Lord God said unto Adam, Because you have hearkened unto the voice of your wife and have eaten of the fruit of the tree of which I commanded you, saying, You shall not eat of it—cursed shall be the ground for your sake: in sorrow you shall eat of it all the days of your life. Thorns, also, and thistles shall it bring forth to you: and you shall eat the herb of the field. By the sweat of your face shall you eat bread, until you shall return unto the ground—for you shall surely die—for out of it you were taken; for dust you were and unto dust you shall return. This was immediately followed by the

fulfillment of what we previously said: Man was driven, or sent, out of Eden.

18. Two important items are shown from the former quotations: First, after man was created, he was not left without intelligence or understanding, to wander in darkness and spend an existence in ignorance and doubt—on the great and important point which affected his happiness—as to the real fact by whom he was created, or unto whom he was amenable for his conduct. God conversed with him face to face: in his presence he was permitted to stand, and from his own mouth he was permitted to receive instruction—he heard his voice, walked before him, and gazed upon his glory while intelligence burst upon his understanding and enabled him to give names to the vast assemblage of his Maker's works.

19. Secondly, we have seen that, though man did transgress, his transgression did not deprive him of the previous knowledge with which he was endowed, relative to the existence and glory of his Creator; for no sooner did he hear his voice than he sought to hide himself from his presence.

20. Having shown, then, in the first instance, that God began to converse with man immediately after he "breathed into his nostrils the breath of life," and that he did not cease to manifest himself to him even after his fall, we shall next proceed to show that, though he was cast out from the Garden of Eden, his knowledge of the existence of God was not lost, neither did God cease to manifest his will unto him.

21. We next proceed to present the account of the direct revelation which man received, after he was cast out of Eden, and further copy from the New Translation [Gen. 3:1–4]:

22. After Adam had been driven out of the garden, he began to till the earth, and to have dominion over all the beasts of the field, and to eat his bread by the sweat of his brow as the Lord had commanded him; and he called upon the name of the Lord, and so did Eve, his wife, also. And they heard the voice of the Lord from the way toward the Garden of Eden speaking unto them; and they saw

him not, for they were shut out from his presence, but he gave unto them commandments that they should worship the Lord their God and should offer the firstlings of their flocks for an offering unto the Lord. And Adam was obedient unto the commandment.

23. And after many days an angel of the Lord appeared unto Adam, saying, Why do you offer sacrifices unto the Lord? And Adam said unto him, I know not, but the Lord commanded me to offer sacrifices.

24. And the angel said unto him, This thing is a similitude of the sacrifice of the Only Begotten of the Father, who is full of grace and truth. And you shall do all that you do in the name of the Son; and you shall repent and call upon God in his name for ever. In that day the holy spirit fell upon Adam and bore record of the Father and the Son.

25. This last quotation, or summary, shows this important fact—that though our first parents were driven out of the Garden of Eden and were even separated from the presence of God by a veil, they still retained a knowledge of his existence, and that sufficiently to move them to call upon him. And further, that no sooner was the plan of redemption revealed to man and he began to call upon God, than the holy spirit was given, bearing record of the Father and Son.

26. Moses also gives us an account in the 3rd chapter of Genesis [Gen. 3:6–9] of the transgression of Cain, and the righteousness of Abel, and of the revelations of God to them. He says: In process of time Cain brought of the fruit of the ground an offering unto the Lord. And Abel also brought of the firstlings of his flock and of the fat thereof. And the Lord had respect unto Abel and to his offering, but unto Cain and to his offering he had not respect. Now Satan knew this and it pleased him. And Cain was very angry and his countenance fell. And the Lord said unto Cain, Why are you angry? Why is your countenance fallen? If you do well, will you not be accepted? And if you do not well, sin lies at the door, and Satan desires to have you, and except you shall hearken unto my commandments, I will deliver you up: and it shall be unto you according to his desire.

27. And Cain went into the field and talked with his brother Abel. And while they were in the field, Cain rose up against his brother Abel and slew him. And Cain gloried in what he had done, saying, I am free! Surely the flocks of my brother will now fall into my hands.

28. But the Lord said unto Cain, Where is Abel, your brother? And he said, I know not. Am I my brother's keeper? And the Lord said, What have you done? The voice of your brother's blood cries unto me from the ground. And now you shall be cursed from the earth which has opened her mouth to receive your brother's blood from your hand. When you till the ground, she shall not henceforth yield unto you her strength. A fugitive, and a vagabond also, you shall be in the earth.

29. And Cain said unto the Lord, Satan tempted me because of my brother's flocks. And I was also angry, for his offering was accepted and mine was not. My punishment is greater than I can bear. Behold, you have driven me out this day from the face of men, and from your face shall I be hid also; and I shall be a fugitive and a vagabond in the earth. And it shall come to pass, everyone that finds me will slay me because of my oath, for these things are not hid from the Lord. And the Lord said unto him, Therefore, whoever slays Cain, vengeance shall be taken on him sevenfold. And the Lord set a mark upon Cain, lest any finding him should kill him.

30. The object of the foregoing quotations is to show to this class the way by which mankind were first made acquainted with the existence of a God: that it was by a manifestation of God to man, and that God continued, after man's transgression, to manifest himself to him and his posterity: and notwithstanding they were separated from his immediate presence that they could not see his face, they continued to hear his voice.

31. Adam, thus being made acquainted with God, communicated the knowledge which he had unto his posterity; and it was through this means that the thought was first suggested to their minds that there was a God, which laid the foundation for the exercise of their faith, through which they could obtain a knowledge of his character and also of his glory.

32. Not only was there a manifestation made unto Adam of the existence of a God, but Moses informs us, as before quoted, that God condescended to talk with Cain after his great transgression in slaying his brother, and that Cain knew that it was the Lord that was talking with him, so that when he was driven out from the presence of his brethren, he carried with him the knowledge of the existence of a God: and through this means, doubtless his posterity became acquainted with the fact that such a being existed.

33. From this we can see that the whole human family, in the early age of their existence, in all their different branches, had this knowledge disseminated among them; so that the existence of God became an object of faith in the early age of the world. And the evidences which these men had of the existence of a God was the testimony of their fathers in the first instance.

34. The reason why we have been thus particular on this part of our subject is that this class may see by what means it was that God became an object of faith among men after the fall, and what it was that stirred up the faith of multitudes to feel after him, to search after a knowledge of his character, perfections, and attributes until they became extensively acquainted with him; and not only commune with him and behold his glory, but be partakers of his power and stand in his presence.

35. Let this class mark particularly that the testimony which these men had of the existence of a God was the testimony of man, for previous to the time that any of Adam's posterity had obtained a manifestation of God to themselves, Adam, their common father, had testified unto them of the existence of God and of his eternal power and Godhead.

36. For instance, Abel, before he received the assurance from Heaven that his offerings were acceptable unto God, had received the important information of his father that such a being did exist, who had created and who did uphold all things. Neither can there be a doubt existing on the mind of any person that Adam was the first who did communicate the knowledge of the existence of a God to his posterity, and that the whole faith of the world, from that

time down to the present, is in a certain degree dependent on the knowledge first communicated to them by their common progenitor; and it has been handed down to the day and generation in which we live, as we shall show from the face of the sacred records.

37. First, Adam was 130 years old when Seth was born (Genesis 5:3) [Gen. 3:15]. And the days of Adam, after he had begotten Seth, were 800 years, making him 930 years old when he died (Gen. 5:4,5) [Gen. 3:15]. Seth was 105 when Enos was born (Gen. 5:6) [Gen. 3:16]; Enos was 90 when Cainan was born (Gen. 5:9) [Gen. 3:19]; Cainan was 70 when Mahalalel was born (5:12) [Gen. 3:20]; Mahalalel was 65 when Jared was born (5:15) [Gen. 3:21]; Jared was 162 when Enoch was born (5:18) [Gen. 3:22]; Enoch was 65 when Methuselah was born (5:21) [Gen. 3:25]; Methuselah was 187 when Lamech was born (5:25) [Gen. 5:3]; Lamech was 182 when Noah was born (5:28) [Gen. 5:4].

38. From this account it appears that Lamech, the ninth from Adam and the father of Noah, was 56 years old when Adam died; Methuselah, 243; Enoch, 308; Jared, 470; Mahalalel, 535; Cainan, 605; Enos, 695; and Seth, 800.

39. So that Lamech, the father of Noah, Methuselah, Enoch, Jared, Mahalalel, Cainan, Enos, Seth, and Adam were all living at the same time and, beyond all controversy, were all preachers of righteousness.

40. Moses further informs us that Seth lived after he begat Enos, 807 years, making him 912 years old at his death (Genesis 5:7,8) [Gen. 3:16,18]. And Enos lived after he begat Cainan, 815 years, making him 905 years old when he died (Gen. 5:10,11) [Gen. 3:19]. And Cainan lived after he begat Mahalalel, 840 years, making him 910 years old at his death (Gen. 5:13,14) [Gen. 3:20]. And Mahalalel lived after he begat Jared, 830 years, making 895 years old when he died (Gen. 5:16,17) [Gen. 3:21]. And Jared lived after he begat Enoch, 800 years, making him 962 years old at his death (Gen. 5:19,20) [Gen. 3:22,24]. And Enoch walked with God, after he begat Methuselah, 300 years, making him 365 years old when he was

translated (Gen. 5:22,23) [Gen. 4:23]. And Methuselah lived after he begat Lamech, 782 years, making him 969 years old when he died (Gen. 5:26,27) [Gen. 5:3]. Lamech lived after he begat Noah, 595 years, making him 777 years old when he died (Gen. 5:30,31) [Gen. 5:4].

41. Agreeably to this account, Adam died in the 930th year of the world, Enoch was translated in the 987th, Seth died in the 1042nd, Enos in the 1140th, Cainan in the 1235th, Mahalalel in the 1290th, Jared in the 1422nd, Lamech in the 1651st, and Methuselah in the 1656th, it being the same year in which the flood came.

42. So that Noah was 84 years old when Enos died, 176 when Cainan died, 234 when Mahalalel died, 366 when Jared died, 595 when Lamech died, and 600 when Methuselah died.

43. We can see from this that Enos, Cainan, Mahalalel, Jared, Methuselah, Lamech, and Noah all lived on the earth at the same time. And that Enos, Cainan, Mahalalel, Jared, Methuselah, and Lamech were all acquainted with both Adam and Noah.

44. From the foregoing it is easily to be seen, not only how the knowledge of God came into the world, but upon what principle it was preserved: that from the time it was first communicated, it was retained in the minds of righteous men who taught not only their own posterity, but the world, so that there was no need of a new revelation to man after Adam's creation to Noah, to give them the first idea or notion of the existence of a God—and not only of a God, but the true and living God.

45. Having traced the chronology of the world from Adam to Noah, we will now trace it from Noah to Abraham. Noah was 502 years old when Shem was born; 98 years afterward the flood came, being the 600th year of Noah's age. And Moses informs us that Noah lived after the flood 350 years, making him 950 years old when he died (Genesis 9:28, 29) [Gen. 5:24].

46. Shem was 100 years old when Arphaxad was born (Genesis 11:10) [Gen. 6:7]. Arphaxad was 35 when Selah was born (Gen.

11:12) [Gen. 6:7]; Selah was 30 when Eber was born (Gen. 11:14) [Gen. 6:7]; Eber was 34 when Peleg was born, in whose days the earth was divided (Gen. 11:16) [Gen. 6:7]; Peleg was 30 when Reu was born (Gen. 11:18) [Gen. 6:7]; Reu was 32 when Serug was born (Gen. 11:20) [Gen. 6:7]; Serug was 30 when Nahor was born (Gen. 11:22) [Gen. 6:7]; Nahor was 29 when Terah was born (Gen. 11:24) [Gen. 6:7]; Terah was 70 when Haran and Abraham were born (Gen. 11:26) [Gen. 6:7].

47. There is some difficulty in the account given by Moses of Abraham's birth. Some have supposed that Abraham was not born until Terah was 130 years old. This conclusion is drawn from a variety of scriptures which are not to our purpose at present to quote. Neither is it a matter of any consequence to us whether Abraham was born when Terah was 70 years old or 130. But in order that there may no doubt exist upon any mind in relation to the object lying immediately before us, in presenting the present chronology we will date the birth of Abraham at the latest period: that is, when Terah was 130 years old. It appears from this account that from the flood to the birth of Abraham was 352 years.

48. Moses informs us that Shem lived after he begat Arphaxad, 500 years (Genesis 11:11) [Gen. 6:7]; this added to 100 years, which was his age when Arphaxad was born, makes him 600 years old when he died. Arphaxad lived, after he begat Selah, 403 years (Gen. 11:13) [Gen. 6:7]; this added to 35 years, which was his age when Selah was born, makes him 438 years old when he died. Selah lived after he begat Eber, 403 years (Gen. 11:15) [Gen. 6:7]; this added to 30 years, which was his age when Eber was born, makes him 433 years old when he died. Eber lived after he begat Peleg, 430 years (Gen. 11:17) [Gen. 6:7]; this added to 34 years, which was his age when Peleg was born, makes him 464 years old. Peleg lived after he begat Reu, 209 years (Gen. 11:19) [Gen. 6:7]; this added to 30 years, which was his age when Reu was born makes him 239 years old when he died. Reu lived after he begat Serug 207 years (Gen. 11:21) [Gen. 6:7]; this added to 32 years, which was his age when Serug was born, makes him 239 years old when he died. Serug lived after he begat Nahor, 200 years (Gen. 11:23) [Gen. 6:7]; this added to 30 years, which was his age when Nahor was born, makes him 230 years old when he

died. Nahor lived after he begat Terah, 119 years (Gen. 11:25) [Gen. 6:7]; this added to 29 years, which was his age when Terah was born, makes him 148 years when he died. Terah was 130 years old when Abraham was born, and is supposed to have lived 75 years after his birth, making him 205 years old when he died.

49. Agreeably to this last account, Peleg died in the 1996th year of the world, Nahor in the 1997th, and Noah in the 2006th. So that Peleg, in whose days the earth was divided, and Nahor, the grandfather of Abraham, both died before Noah: the former being 239 years old and the latter 148. And who cannot but see that they must have had a long and intimate acquaintance with Noah?

50. Reu died in the 2026th year of the world, Serug in the 2049th, Terah in the 2083rd, Arphaxad in the 2096th, Selah in the 2126th, Shem in the 2158th, Abraham in the 2183rd, and Eber in the 2187th, which was 4 years after Abraham's death. And Eber was the fourth from Noah.

51. Nahor, Abraham's brother, was 58 years old when Noah died, Terah 128, Serug 187, Reu 219, Eber 283, Selah 313, Arphaxad 344, and Shem 448.

52. It appears from this account, that Nahor, brother of Abraham, Terah, Nahor, Serug, Reu, Peleg, Eber, Selah, Arphaxad, Shem, and Noah all lived on the earth at the same time. And that Abraham was 18 years old when Reu died, 41 when Serug and his brother Nahor died, 75 when Terah died, 88 when Arphaxad died, 118 when Selah died, 150 when Shem died, and that Eber lived 4 years after Abraham's death. And that Shem, Arphaxad, Selah, Eber, Reu, Serug, Terah, and Nahor, the brother of Abraham, and Abraham, lived at the same time. And that Nahor, brother of Abraham, Terah, Serug, Reu, Eber, Selah, Arphaxad, and Shem, were all acquainted with both Noah and Abraham.

53. We have now traced the chronology of the world, agreeably to the account given in our present Bible, from Adam to Abraham, and have clearly determined, beyond the power of controversy, that there was no difficulty in preserving the knowledge of God in the

world from the creation of Adam, and the manifestation made to his immediate descendants, as set forth in the former part of this lecture, so that the students in this class need not have any dubiety resting on their minds on this subject; for they can easily see that it is impossible for it to be otherwise, but that the knowledge of the existence of a God must have continued from father to son as a matter of tradition, at least. For we cannot suppose that a knowledge of this important fact could have existed in the mind of any of the before-mentioned individuals without their having made it known to their posterity.

54. We have now shown how it was that the first thought ever existed in the mind of any individual that there was such a being as a God, who had created and did uphold all things: that it was by reason of the manifestation which he first made to our father Adam, when he stood in his presence and conversed with him face to face, at the time of his creation.

55. Let us here observe that after any portion of the human family are made acquainted with the important fact that there is a God who has created and does uphold all things, the extent of their knowledge, respecting his character and glory, will depend upon their diligence and faithfulness in seeking after him, until like Enoch, the brother of Jared, and Moses, they shall obtain faith in God and power with him to behold him face to face.

56. We have now clearly set forth how it is, and how it was, that God became an object of faith for rational beings, and also upon what foundation the testimony was based, which excited the inquiry and diligent search of the ancient saints to seek after and obtain a knowledge of the glory of God. And we have seen that it was human testimony, and human testimony only, that excited this inquiry in the first instance in their minds—it was the credence they gave to the testimony of their fathers—this testimony having aroused their minds to inquire after the knowledge of God, the inquiry frequently terminated, indeed always terminated, when rightly pursued, in the most glorious discoveries and Eternal certainty.

Questions and Answers on the Foregoing Principles

57. Question 1: Is there a being who has faith in himself independently?
Answer: There is.

58. Question 2: Who is it?
A: It is God.

59. Question 3: How do you prove that God has faith in himself independently?
A: Because he is omnipotent, omnipresent, and omniscient, without beginning of days or end of life, and in him all fullness dwells. Ephesians 1:23 [Eph. 1:3]: Which is his body, the fullness of him that filleth all in all. Colossians 1:19 [Col. 1:4]: For it pleased the Father that in him should all fullness dwell (¶12).

60. Question 4: Is he the object in whom the faith of all other rational and accountable beings centers for life and salvation?
A: He is.

61. Question 5: How do you prove it?
A: Isaiah 45:22 [Isa. 15:19]: Look unto me, and be ye saved, all the ends of the earth: for I am God and there is none else. Romans 11:34–36 [Rom. 1:58]: For who hath known the mind of the Lord? Or who hath been his counselor? Or who hath first given to him, and it shall be recompensed unto him again? For of him, and through him, and to him, are all things: to whom be glory for ever. Amen. Isaiah 40:9–17 [Isa. 14:2–3]: O Zion that bringest good tidings (or, O thou that tellest good tidings to Zion), get thee up into the high mountain: O Jerusalem, that bringest good tidings (or, O thou that tellest good tidings to Jerusalem), lift up thy voice with strength; lift it up, be not afraid; say unto the cities of Judah, Behold your God! Behold the Lord your God will come with strong hand [or, against the strong] and his arm shall rule for him: behold, his reward is with him and his work before him (or, recompense for his work). He shall feed his flock like a shepherd: he shall gather his lambs with his arms, and carry them in his bosom, and shall gently lead those that are with young. Who hath measured the waters in the hollow of his hand, and meted out heaven with the span, and comprehended the dust of the earth in a measure, weighed the

mountains in scales and the hills in a balance? Who hath directed the spirit of the Lord or, being his counselor, hath taught him? With whom took he counsel, and who instructed him, and taught him in the path of judgment, and taught him knowledge, and shewed to him the way of understanding? Behold, the nations are as a drop of a bucket and are counted as the small dust of the balance; behold, he taketh up the isles as a very little thing. And Lebanon is not sufficient to burn, nor the beasts thereof sufficient for a burnt offering. All nations are before him as nothing, and they are counted to him less than nothing and vanity. Jeremiah 51:15,16 [Jer. 18:13]: He (the Lord) hath made the earth by his power, he hath established the world by his wisdom, and hath stretched out the Heaven by his understanding. When he uttereth his voice there is a multitude of waters in the heavens; and he causeth the vapors to ascend from the ends of the earth: He maketh lightnings with rain, and bringeth forth the wind out of his treasures. 1 Corinthians 8:6 [1 Cor. 1:32]: But to us there is but one God, the Father, of whom are all things, and we in him, and one Lord Jesus Christ, by whom are all things, and we by him (¶12).

62. Question 6: How did men first come to the knowledge of the existence of a God, so as to exercise faith in him?
A: In order to answer this question, it will be necessary to go back and examine man at his creation, the circumstances in which he was placed, and the knowledge which he had of God (¶¶3–11).

63. First, when man was created he stood in the presence of God (Genesis 1:27,28) [Gen. 2:8–9]. From this we learn that man, at his creation, stood in the presence of his God, and had most perfect knowledge of his existence.

64. Secondly, God conversed with him after his transgression (Genesis 3:8–22) [Gen. 2:17–19] (¶¶13–17). From this we learn that, though man did transgress, he was not deprived of the previous knowledge which he had of the existence of God (¶19).

65. Thirdly, God conversed with man after he cast him out of the garden (¶¶22–25).

66. Fourthly, God also conversed with Cain after he had slain Abel (Genesis 4:4–6) [Gen. 3:8] (¶¶ 26–29).

67. Question 7: What is the object of the foregoing quotation?
A: It is that it may be clearly seen how it was that the first thoughts were suggested to the minds of men of the existence of God, and how extensively this knowledge was spread among the immediate descendants of Adam (¶¶ 30–33).

68. Question 8: What testimony had the immediate descendants of Adam in proof of the existence of a God?
A: The testimony of their father. And after they were made acquainted with his existence by the testimony of their father, they were dependent upon the exercise of their own faith for a knowledge of his character, perfections, and attributes (¶¶ 23–26).

69. Question 9: Had any others of the human family, besides Adam, a knowledge of the existence of God, in the first instance, by any other means than human testimony?
A: They had not. For previous to the time that they could have power to obtain a manifestation for themselves, the all-important fact had been communicated to them by their common father: and so, from father to child, the knowledge was communicated as extensively as the knowledge of his existence was known; for it was by this means, in the first instance, that men had a knowledge of his existence (¶¶ 35, 36).

70. Question 10: How do you know that the knowledge of the existence of God was communicated in this manner throughout the different ages of the world?
A: By the chronology obtained through the revelations of God.

71. Question 11: How would you divide that chronology in order to convey it to the understanding clearly?
A: Into two parts: First, by embracing that period of the world from Adam to Noah, and secondly, from Noah to Abraham, from which period the knowledge of the existence of God has been so general that it is a matter of no dispute in what manner the idea of his existence has been retained in the world.

72. Question 12: How many noted righteous men lived from Adam to Noah?
A: Nine, which includes Abel, who was slain by his brother.

73. Question 13: What are their names?
A: Abel, Seth, Enos, Cainan, Mahalalel, Jared, Enoch, Methuselah, and Lamech.

74. Question 14: How old was Adam when Seth was born?
A: One hundred and thirty years (Genesis 5:3) [Gen. 3:15].

75. Question 15: How many years did Adam live after Seth was born?
A: Eight hundred (Genesis 5:4) [Gen. 3:15].

76. Question 16: How old was Adam when he died?
A: Nine hundred and thirty years (Genesis 5:5) [Gen. 3:15].

77. Question 17: How old was Seth when Enos was born?
A: One hundred and five years (Genesis 5:6) [Gen. 3:16].

78. Question 18: How old was Enos when Cainan was born?
A: Ninety years (Genesis 5:9) [Gen. 3:19].

79. Question 19: How old was Cainan when Mahalalel was born?
A: Seventy years (Genesis 5:12) [Gen. 3:20].

80. Question 20: How old was Mahalalel when Jared was born?
A: Sixty-five years (Genesis 5:15) [Gen. 3:21].

81. Question 21: How old was Jared when Enoch was born?
A: One hundred and sixty-two years (Genesis 5:18) [Gen. 3:22].

82. Question 22: How old was Enoch when Methuselah was born?
A: Sixty-five (Genesis 5:21) [Gen. 3:25].

83. Question 23: How old was Methuselah when Lamech was born?
A: One hundred and eighty-seven years (Genesis 5:25) [Gen. 5:3].

84. Question 24: How old was Lamech when Noah was born?
A: One hundred and eighty-two years (Genesis 5:28) [Gen. 5:4]. For this chronology see (¶37).

85. Question 25: How many years, according to this account, was it from Adam to Noah?
A: One thousand and fifty-six years.

86. Question 26: How old was Lamech when Adam died?
A: Lamech, the ninth from Adam (including Abel), and father of Noah, was fifty-six years old when Adam died.

87. Question 27: How old was Methuselah?
A: Two hundred and forty-three years.

88. Question 28: How old was Enoch?
A: Three hundred and eight years.

89. Question 29: How old was Jared?
A: Four hundred and seventy years.

90. Question 30: How old was Mahalalel?
A: Five hundred and thirty-five.

91. Question 31: How old was Cainan?
A: Six hundred and five years.

92. Question 32: How old was Enos?
A: Six hundred and ninety-five years.

93. Question 33: How old was Seth?
A: Eight hundred. For this item of the account see (¶38).

94. Question 34: How many of these noted men were contemporary with Adam?
A: Nine.

95. Question 35: What are their names?

A: Abel, Seth, Enos, Cainan, Mahalalel, Jared, Enoch, Methuselah, and Lamech (¶39).

96. Question 36: How long did Seth live after Enos was born?
A: Eight hundred and seven years (Genesis 5:7) [Gen. 3:16].

97. Question 37: What was Seth's age when he died?
A: Nine hundred and twelve years (Genesis 5:8) [Gen. 3:18].

98. Question 38: How long did Enos live after Cainan was born?
A: Eight hundred and fifteen years (Genesis 5:10) [Gen. 3:19].

99. Question 39: What was Enos's age when he died?
A: Nine hundred and five years (Genesis 5:11) [Gen. 3:19].

100. Question 40: How long did Cainan live after Mahalalel was born?
A: Eight hundred and forty years (Genesis 5:13) [Gen. 3:20].

101. Question 41: What was Cainan's age when he died?
A: Nine hundred and ten years (Genesis 5:14) [Gen. 3:20].

102. Question 42: How long did Mahalalel live after Jared was born?
A: Eight hundred and thirty years (Genesis 5:16) [Gen. 3:21].

103. Question 43: What was Mahalalel's age when he died?
A: Eight hundred and ninety-five years (Genesis 5:17) [Gen. 3:21].

104. Question 44: How long did Jared live after Enoch was born?
A: Eight hundred years (Genesis 5:19) [Gen. 3:22].

105. Question 45: What was Jared's age when he died?
A: Nine hundred and sixty-two years (Genesis 5:20) [Gen. 3:24].

106. Question 46: How long did Enoch walk with God after Methuselah was born?
A: Three hundred years (Genesis 5:22) [Gen. 4:23].

107. Question 47: What was Enoch's age when he was translated?

A: Three hundred and sixty-five years (Genesis 5:23) [Gen. 4:23].

108. Question 48: How long did Methuselah live after Lamech was born?
A: Seven hundred and eighty-two years (Genesis 5:26) [Gen. 5:3].

109. Question 49: What was Methuselah's age when he died?
A: Nine hundred and sixty-nine years (Genesis 5:27) [Gen. 5:3].

110. Question 50: How long did Lamech live after Noah was born?
A: Five hundred and ninety-five years (Genesis 5:30) [Gen. 5:4].

111. Question 51: What was Lamech's age when he died?
A: Seven hundred and seventy-seven years (Genesis 5:31) [Gen. 5:4]. For the account of the last item see (¶40).

112. Question 52: In what year of the world did Adam die?
A: In the nine hundred and thirtieth.

113. Question 53: In what year was Enoch translated?
A: In the nine hundred and eighty-seventh.

114. Question 54: In what year did Seth die?
A: In the one thousand and forty-second.

115. Question 55: In what year did Enos die?
A: In the eleven hundred and fortieth.

116. Question 56: In what year did Cainan die?
A: In the twelve hundred and thirty-fifth.

117. Question 57: In what year did Mahalalel die?
A: In the twelve hundred and ninetieth.

118. Question 58: In what year did Jared die?
A: In the fourteen hundred and twenty-second.

119. Question 59: In what year did Lamech die?
A: In the sixteen hundred and fifty-first.

120. Question 60: In what year did Methuselah die?
A: In the sixteen hundred and fifty-sixth. For this account see (¶41).

121. Question 61: How old was Noah when Enos died?
A: Eighty-four years.

122. Question 62: How old when Cainan died?
A: One hundred and seventy-nine years.

123. Question 63: How old when Mahalalel died?
A: Two hundred and thirty-four years.

124. Question 64: How old when Jared died?
A: Three hundred and sixty-six years.

125. Question 65: How old when Lamech died?
A: Five hundred and ninety-five years.

126. Question 66: How old when Methuselah died?
A: Six hundred years. See (¶42) for the last item.

127. Question 67: How many of those men lived in the days of Noah?
A: Six.

128. Question 68: What are their names?
A: Seth, Enos, Cainan, Mahalalel, Jared, Methuselah, and Lamech (¶43).

129. Question 69: How many of those men were contemporary with Adam and Noah both?
A: Six.

130. Question 70: What are their names?
A: Enos, Cainan, Mahalalel, Jared, Methuselah, and Lamech (¶43).

131. Question 71: According to the foregoing account, how was the knowledge of the existence of God first suggested to the minds of men?

A: By the manifestation made to our father Adam when he was in the presence of God, both before and while he was in Eden (¶44).

132. Question 72: How was the knowledge of the existence of God disseminated among the inhabitants of the world?
A: By tradition from father to son (¶44).

133. Question 73: How old was Noah when Shem was born?
A: Five hundred and two years (Genesis 5:32) [Gen. 5:5], (Gen. 11:10) [Gen. 6:7].

134. Question 74: What was the term of years from the birth of Shem to the flood?
A: Ninety-eight.

135. Question 75: What was the term of years that Noah lived after the flood?
A: Three hundred and fifty (Genesis 9:28) [Gen. 5:24].

136. Question 76: What was Noah's age when he died?
A: Nine hundred and fifty years (Genesis 9:29) [Gen. 5:24].

137. Question 77: What was Shem's age when Arphaxad was born?
A: One hundred years (Genesis 11:10) [Gen. 6:7].

138. Question 78: What was Arphaxad's age when Selah was born?
A: Thirty-five years (Genesis 11:12) [Gen. 6:7].

139. Question 79: What was Selah's age when Eber was born?
A: Thirty (Genesis 11:14) [Gen. 6:7].

140. Question 80: What was Eber's age when Peleg was born?
A: Thirty-four years (Genesis 11:16) [Gen. 6:7].

141. Question 81: What was Peleg's age when Reu was born?
A: Thirty years (Genesis 11:18) [Gen. 6:7].

142. Question 82: What was Reu's age when Serug was born?
A: Thirty-two years (Genesis 11:20) [Gen. 6:7].

143. Question 83: What was Serug's age when Nahor was born?
A: Thirty years (Genesis 11:22) [Gen. 6:7].

144. Question 84: What was Nahor's age when Terah was born?
A: Twenty-nine years (Genesis 11:24) [Gen. 6:7].

145. Question 85: What was Terah's age when Nahor (the brother of Abraham) was born?
A: Seventy years (Genesis 11:26) [Gen. 6:7].

146. Question 86: What was Terah's age when Abraham was born?
A: Some suppose one hundred and thirty years, and others seventy (Genesis 11:26) [Gen. 6:7] (¶46).

147. Question 87: What was the number of years from the flood to the birth of Abraham?
A: Supposing Abraham to have been born when Terah was one hundred and thirty years old, it was three hundred and fifty-two years, but if he were born when Terah was seventy years old, it was two hundred and ninety-two years (¶47).

148. Question 88: How long did Shem live after Arphaxad was born?
A: Five hundred years (Genesis 11:11) [Gen. 6:7].

149. Question 89: What was Shem's age when he died?
A: Six hundred years (Genesis 11:11) [Gen. 6:7].

150. Question 90: What number of years did Arphaxad live after Selah was born?
A: Four hundred and three years (Genesis 11:13) [Gen. 6:7].

151. Question 91: What was Arphaxad's age when he died?
A: Four hundred and thirty-eight years.

152. Question 92: What number of years did Selah live after Eber was born?
A: Four hundred and three years (Genesis 11:15) [Gen. 6:7].

153. Question 93: What was Selah's age when he died?
A: Four hundred and thirty-three years.

154. Question 94: What number of years did Eber live after Peleg was born?
A: Four hundred and thirty years (Genesis 11:17) [Gen. 6:7].

155. Question 95: What was Eber's age when he died?
A: Four hundred and sixty-four years.

156. Question 96: What number of years did Peleg live after Reu was born?
A: Two hundred and nine years (Genesis 11:19) [Gen. 6:7].

157. Question 97: What was Peleg's age when he died?
A: Two hundred and thirty-nine years.

158. Question 98: What number of years did Reu live after Serug was born?
A: Two hundred and seven years (Genesis 11:21) [Gen. 6:7].

159. Question 99: What was Reu's age when he died?
A: Two hundred and thirty-nine years.

160. Question 100: What number of years did Serug live after Nahor was born?
A: Two hundred years (Genesis 11:23) [Gen. 6:7].

161. Question 101: What was Serug's age when he died?
A: Two hundred and thirty years.

162. Question 102: What number of years did Nahor live after Terah was born?
A: One hundred and nineteen years (Genesis 11:25) [Gen. 6:7].

163. Question 103: What was Nahor's age when he died?
A: One hundred and forty-eight years.

164. Question 104: What number of years did Terah live after Abraham was born?
A: Supposing Terah to have been one hundred and thirty years old when Abraham was born, he lived seventy-five years, but if Abraham was born when Terah was seventy years old, he lived one hundred and thirty-five.

165. Question 105: What was Terah's age when he died?
A: Two hundred and five years (Genesis 11:32) [Gen. 6:8]. For this account from the birth of Arphaxad to the death of Terah, see (¶48).

166. Question 106: In what year of the world did Peleg die?
A: Agreeably to the foregoing chronology, he died in the nineteen hundred and ninety-sixth year of the world.

167. Question 107: In what year of the world did Nahor die?
A: In the nineteen hundred and ninety-seventh.

168. Question 108: In what year of the world did Noah die?
A: In the two thousand and sixth.

169. Question 109: In what year of the world did Reu die?
A: In the two thousand and twenty-sixth.

170. Question 110: In what year of the world did Serug die?
A: In the two thousand and forty-ninth.

171. Question 111: In what year of the world did Terah die?
A: In the two thousand and eighty-third.

172. Question 112: In what year of the world did Arphaxad die?
A: In the two thousand and ninety-sixth.

173. Question 113: In what year of the world did Selah die?
A: In the twenty one hundred and twenty-sixth.

174. Question 114: In what year of the world did Abraham die?
A: In the twenty one hundred and eighty-third.

175. Question 115: In what year of the world did Eber die?
A: In the twenty one hundred and eighty-seventh. For this account of the year of the world in which those men died, see (¶¶49–50).

176. Question 116: How old was Nahor, Abraham's brother, when Noah died?
A: Fifty-eight years.

177. Question 117: How old was Terah?
A: One hundred and twenty-eight.

178. Question 118: How old was Serug?
A: One hundred and eighty-seven.

179. Question 119: How old was Reu?
A: Two hundred and nineteen.

180. Question 120: How old was Eber?
A: Two hundred and eighty-three.

181. Question 121: How old was Selah?
A: Three hundred and thirteen.

182. Question 122: How old was Arphaxad?
A: Three hundred and forty-eight.

183. Question 123: How old was Shem?
A: Four hundred and forty-eight. For the last account, see (¶51).

184. Question 124: How old was Abraham when Reu died?
A: Eighteen years, if he were born when Terah was one hundred and thirty years old.

185. Question 125: What was his age when Serug and Nahor, Abraham's brother, died?
A: Forty-one years.

186. Question 126: What was his age when Terah died?
A: Seventy-five years.

187. Question 127: What was his age when Arphaxad died?
A: Eighty-eight.

188. Question 128: What was his age when Selah died?
A: One hundred and eighteen years.

189. Question 129: What was his age when Shem died?
A: One hundred and fifty years. For this see (¶52).

190. Question 130: How many noted characters lived from Noah to Abraham?
A: Ten.

191. Question 131: What are their names?
A: Shem, Arphaxad, Selah, Eber, Peleg, Reu, Serug, Nahor, Terah, and Nahor, Abraham's brother (¶52).

192. Question 132: How many of these were contemporary with Noah?
A: The whole.

193. Question 133: How many with Abraham?
A: Eight.

194. Question 134: What are their names?
A: Nahor, Abraham's brother, Terah, Serug, Reu, Eber, Selah, Arphaxad, and Shem.(¶52).

195. Question 135: How many were contemporary with both Noah and Abraham?
A: Eight.

196. Question 136: What are their names?
A: Shem, Arphaxad, Selah, Eber, Reu, Serug, Terah, and Nahor, Abraham's brother (¶52).

197. Question 137: Did any of these men die before Noah?
A: They did.

198. Question 138: Who were they?
A: Peleg, in whose days the earth was divided, and Nahor, Abraham's grandfather (¶49).

199. Question 139: Did any one of them live longer than Abraham?
A: There was one (¶50).

200. Question 140: Who was it?
A: Eber, the fourth from Noah (¶50).

201. Question 141: In whose days was the earth divided?
A: In the days of Peleg.

202. Question 142: Where have we the account given that the earth was divided in the days of Peleg?
A: Genesis 10:25 [Gen. 6:4].

203. Question 143: Can you repeat the sentence?
A: Unto Eber were born two sons; the name on one was Peleg, for in his days the earth was divided.

204. Question 144: What testimony have men, in the first instance, that there is a God?
A: Human testimony and human testimony only (¶56).

205. Question 145: What excited the ancient saints to seek diligently after a knowledge of the glory of God, his perfections, and attributes?
A: The credence they gave to the testimony of their fathers (¶56).

206. Question 146: How do men obtain a knowledge of the glory of God, his perfections, and attributes?
A: By devoting themselves to his service, through prayer and supplication incessantly, strengthening their faith in him, until like Enoch, the brother of Jared, and Moses, they obtain a manifestation of God to themselves (¶55).

207. Question 147: Is the knowledge of the existence of God a matter of mere tradition, founded upon human testimony alone, until a person receives a manifestation of God to themselves?
A: It is.

208. Question 148: How do you prove it?
A: From the whole of the first and second lectures.

[See Appendix: Timeline of the Fathers]

LECTURE THIRD

Of Faith

1. In the second lecture it was shown how it was that the knowledge of the existence of God came into the world, and by what means the first thoughts were suggested to the minds of men that such a being did actually exist. And that it was by reason of the knowledge of his existence that there was a foundation laid for the exercise of faith in him as the only being in whom faith could center for life and salvation. For faith could not center in a being of whose existence we had no idea, because the idea of his existence in the first instance is essential to the exercise of faith in him. Romans 10:14 [Rom. 1:49]: How then shall they call on him in whom they have not believed? And how shall they believe in him of whom they have not heard? And how shall they hear without a preacher (or one sent to tell them)? So then faith comes by hearing the word of God (New Translation).

2. Let us here observe that three things are necessary in order that any rational and intelligent being may exercise faith in God unto life and salvation.

3. First, the idea that he actually exists.

4. Secondly, a correct idea of his character, perfections, and attributes.

5. Thirdly, an actual knowledge that the course of life which he is pursuing is according to his will. For without an acquaintance with these three important facts, the faith of every rational being must be imperfect and unproductive, but with this understanding it can become perfect and fruitful, abounding in righteousness unto the praise and glory of God the Father and the Lord Jesus Christ.

6. Having previously been made acquainted with the way the idea of his existence came into the world, as well as the fact of his existence, we shall proceed to examine his character, perfections, and attributes, in order that this class may see not only the just grounds which they have for the exercise of faith in him for life and

salvation, but the reasons that all the world also, as far as the idea of his existence extends, may have to exercise faith in him, the Father of all living.

7. As we have been indebted to a revelation which God made of himself to his creatures, in the first instance, for the idea of his existence, so in like manner we are indebted to the revelations which he has given to us for a correct understanding of his character, perfections, and attributes, because without the revelations which he has given to us, no man by searching could find out God. Job 11:7–9 [Job 5:2]. 1 Corinthians 2:9–11 [1 Cor. 1:8]: But as it is written: Eye has not seen, nor ear heard, neither have entered into the heart of man, the things which God has prepared for them that love him, but God has revealed them unto us by his spirit: for the spirit searches all things, yea, the deep things of God. For what man knows the things of a man save the spirit of man which is in him? Even so, the things of God no man knows but by the spirit of God.

8. Having said so much, we proceed to examine the character which the revelations have given of God.

9. Moses gives us the following account in Exodus 34:6 [Exo. 18:6]: And the Lord passed by before him and proclaimed, The Lord God, the Lord God, merciful and gracious, long-suffering and abundant in goodness and truth. Psalms 103:6 – 8 [Ps. 103:1]: The Lord executes righteousness and judgment for all that are oppressed. He made known his ways unto Moses, his acts unto the children of Israel. The Lord is merciful and gracious, slow to anger and plenteous in mercy. Psalms 103:17,18 [Ps. 103:2]: But the mercy of the Lord is from everlasting to everlasting upon them that fear him, and his righteousness unto children's children, to such as keep his covenant and to those that remember his commandments to do them. Psalms 90:2 [Ps. 90:1]: Before the mountains were brought forth, or ever you had formed the earth and the world, even from everlasting to everlasting, you are God. Hebrews 1:10–12 [Heb. 1:2]: And you, Lord, in the beginning have laid the foundation of the earth and the heavens are the works of your hands: they shall perish, but you shall remain; and they shall wax old as a garment,

and as a vesture shall you fold them up, and they shall be changed, but you are the same and your years shall not fail. James 1:17 [Epistle of Jacob 1:5]: Every good gift and every perfect gift is from above and comes down from the Father of Lights, with whom is no variableness, neither shadow of turning. Malachi 3:6 [Mal. 1:6]: For I am the Lord, I change not; therefore, ye sons of Jacob are not consumed.

10. Book of Commandments, chapt. 2nd, commencing in the third line of the first paragraph [JSH 10:2]: For God doth not walk in crooked paths, neither doth he turn to the right hand nor to the left, neither doth he vary from that which he hath said, therefore his paths are straight and his course is one eternal round. Book of Commandments, chapt. 37:1 [T&C 18:1]: Listen to the voice of the Lord your God, even Alpha and Omega, the Beginning and the End, whose course is one eternal round, the same today as yesterday and for ever.

11. Numbers 23:19 [Num. 10:24]: God is not a man that he should lie, neither the son of man that he should repent. 1 John 4:8 [1 John 1:19]: He that loves not knows not God, for God is love. Acts 10:34 [Acts 6:7]: Then Peter opened his mouth and said, Of a truth I perceive that God is no respecter of persons, but in every nation, he that fears God and works righteousness is accepted with him.

12. From the foregoing testimonies we learn the following things respecting the character of God:

13. First, that he was God before the world was created, and the same God that he was after it was created.

14. Secondly, that he is merciful and gracious, slow to anger, abundant in goodness, and that he was so from everlasting and will be to everlasting.

15. Thirdly, that he changes not, neither is there variableness with him, but that he is the same from everlasting to everlasting, being the same yesterday, today, and for ever; and that his course is one eternal round, without variation.

16. Fourthly, that he is a God of truth and cannot lie.

17. Fifthly, that he is no respecter of persons, but in every nation he that fears God and works righteousness is accepted of him.

18. Sixthly, that he is love.

19. An acquaintance with these attributes in the divine character is essentially necessary in order that the faith of any rational being can center in him for life and salvation. For if he did not in the first instance believe him to be God, that is, the creator and upholder of all things, he could not center his faith in him for life and salvation, for fear there should be a greater than he who would thwart all his plans, and he, like the gods of the heathen, would be unable to fulfill his promises. But seeing he is God over all, from everlasting to everlasting, the creator and upholder of all things, no such fear can exist in the minds of those who put their trust in him, so that in this respect their faith can be without wavering.

20. But secondly: unless he was merciful and gracious, slow to anger, long-suffering, and full of goodness, such is the weakness of human nature and so great the frailties and imperfections of men that unless they believed that these excellencies existed in the divine character, the faith necessary to salvation could not exist. For doubt would take the place of faith, and those who know their weakness and liability to sin would be in constant doubt of salvation, if it were not for the idea which they have of the excellency of the character of God: that he is slow to anger, and long-suffering, and of a forgiving disposition, and does forgive iniquity, transgression, and sin. An idea of these facts does away doubt and makes faith exceedingly strong.

21. But it is equally as necessary that men should have the idea that he is a God who changes not in order to have faith in him as it is to have the idea that he is gracious and long-suffering. For without the idea of unchangeableness in the character of the Deity, doubt would take the place of faith. But with the idea that he changes not, faith lays hold upon the excellencies in his character with unshaken

confidence, believing he is the same yesterday, today, and for ever, and that his course is one eternal round.

22. And again, the idea that he is a God of truth and cannot lie is equally as necessary to the exercise of faith in him as the idea of his unchangeableness. For without the idea that he was a God of truth and could not lie, the confidence necessary to be placed in his word in order to the exercise of faith in him could not exist. But having the idea that he is not man that he can lie, it gives power to the minds of men to exercise faith in him.

23. But it is also necessary that men should have an idea that he is no respecter of persons, for with the idea of all the other excellencies in his character and this one wanting, men could not exercise faith in him; because if he were a respecter of persons, they could not tell what their privileges were, nor how far they were authorized to exercise faith in him, or whether they were authorized to do it at all; but all must be confusion. But no sooner are the minds of men made acquainted with the truth on this point —that he is no respecter of persons—than they see that they have authority by faith to lay hold on eternal life, the richest boon of Heaven, because God is no respecter of persons and that every man in every nation has an equal privilege.

24. And lastly, but not less important to the exercise of faith in God, is the idea that he is love, for with all the other excellencies in his character, without this one to influence them, they could not have such powerful dominion over the minds of men. But when the idea is planted in the mind that he is love, who cannot see the just ground that men of every nation, kindred, and tongue have to exercise faith in God so as to obtain eternal life?

25. From the above description of the character of the Deity which is given him in the revelations to men, there is a sure foundation for the exercise of faith in him among every people, nation, and kindred, from age to age, and from generation to generation.

26. Let us here observe that the foregoing is the character which is given of God in his revelations to the Former Day Saints, and it is

also the character which is given of him in his revelations to the Latter Day Saints, so that the saints of former days and those of latter days are both alike in this respect; the "Latter Day Saints" having as good grounds to exercise faith in God as the former day saints had because the same character is given of him to both.

Questions and Answers on the Foregoing Principles

27. Question 1: What was shown in the second lecture?
Answer: It was shown how the knowledge of the existence of God came into the world (¶1).

28. Question 2: What is the effect of the idea of his existence among men?
A: It lays the foundation for the exercise of faith in him (¶1).

29. Question 3: Is the idea of his existence, in the first instance, necessary in order for the exercise of faith in him?
A: It is (¶1).

30. Question 4: How do you prove it?
A: Romans 10:14 [Rom. 1:49] (¶1).

31. Question 5: How many things are necessary for us to understand, respecting the Deity and our relation to him, in order that we may exercise faith in him for life and salvation?
A: Three (¶2).

32. Question 6: What are they?
A: First, that God does actually exist. Secondly, correct ideas of his character, his perfections, and attributes. And thirdly, that the course which we pursue is according to his mind and will (¶¶3–5).

33. Question 7: Would the idea of any one or two of the above-mentioned things enable a person to exercise faith in God?
A: It would not, for without the idea of them all, faith would be imperfect and unproductive (¶5).

34. Question 8: Would an idea of these three things lay a sure foundation for the exercise of faith in God so as to obtain life and salvation?
A: It would, for by the idea of these three things, faith could become perfect and fruitful, abounding in righteousness unto the praise and glory of God (¶5).

35. Question 9: How are we to be made acquainted with the before-mentioned things respecting the Deity, and respecting ourselves?
A: By revelation (¶6).

36. Question 10: Could these things be found out by any other means than by revelation?
A: They could not.

37. Question 11: How do you prove it?
A: By the scriptures: Job 11:7–9 [Job 5:2]; 1 Corinthians 2:9–11 [1 Cor. 1:8] (¶7).

38. Question 12: What things do we learn in the revelations of God respecting his character?
A: We learn the six following things: First, that he was God before the world was created and the same God that he was after it was created. Secondly, that he is merciful and gracious, slow to anger, abundant in goodness, and that he was so from everlasting, and will be so to everlasting. Thirdly, that he changes not, neither is there variableness with him, and that his course is one eternal round. Fourthly, that he is a God of truth and cannot lie. Fifthly, that he is no respecter of persons. And Sixthly, that he is love (¶¶12–18).

39. Question 13: Where do you find the revelations which give us this idea of the character of the Deity?
A: In the Bible and Book of Commandments, and they are quoted in the third lecture (¶¶9–11).

40. Question 14: What effect would it have on any rational being not to have an idea that the Lord was God, the creator and upholder of all things?

A: It would prevent him from exercising faith in him unto life and salvation.

41. Question 15: Why would it prevent him from exercising faith in God?
A: Because he would be as the heathen, not knowing but there might be a being greater and more powerful than he, and thereby he be prevented from fulfilling his promises (¶19).

42. Question 16: Does this idea prevent this doubt?
A: It does, for persons having this idea are enabled thereby to exercise faith without this doubt (¶19).

43. Question 17: Is it not also necessary to have the idea that God is merciful and gracious, long-suffering and full of goodness?
A: It is (¶20).

44. Question 18: Why is it necessary?
A: Because of the weakness and imperfections of human nature and the great frailties of man; for such is the weakness of man and such his frailties that he is liable to sin continually, and if God were not long-suffering and full of compassion, gracious and merciful, and of a forgiving disposition, man would be cut off from before him, in consequence of which he would be in continual doubt and could not exercise faith: for where doubt is, there faith has no power. But by man's believing that God is full of compassion and forgiveness, long-suffering and slow to anger, he can exercise faith in him and overcome doubt so as to be exceedingly strong (¶20).

45. Question 19: Is it not equally as necessary that man should have an idea that God changes not, neither is there variableness with him, in order to exercise faith in him unto life and salvation?
A: It is, because without this, he would not know how soon the mercy of God might change into cruelty, his long-suffering into rashness, his love into hatred, and in consequence of which doubt man would be incapable of exercising faith in him. But having the idea that he is unchangeable, man can have faith in him continually, believing that what he was yesterday he is today and will be for ever (¶21).

46. Question 20: Is it not necessary also for men to have an idea that God is a being of truth before they can have perfect faith in him?
A: It is, for unless men have this idea, they cannot place confidence in his word, and not being able to place confidence in his word, they could not have faith in him. But believing that he is a God of truth and that his word cannot fail, their faith can rest in him without doubt (¶22).

47. Question 21: Could man exercise faith in God so as to obtain eternal life unless he believed that God was no respecter of persons?
A: He could not, because without this idea he could not certainly know that it was his privilege so to do, and in consequence of this doubt his faith could not be sufficiently strong to save him (¶23).

48. Question 22: Would it be possible for a man to exercise faith in God so as to be saved unless he had an idea that God was love?
A: He could not, because man could not love God unless he had an idea that God was love, and if he did not love God, he could not have faith in him (¶24).

49. Question 23: What is the description, which the sacred writers give of the character of the Deity, calculated to do?
A: It is calculated to lay a foundation for the exercise of faith in him, as far as the knowledge extends among all people, tongues, languages, kindreds, and nations, and that from age to age and from generation to generation (¶25).

50. Question 24: Is the character which God has given of himself uniform?
A: It is, in all his revelations, whether to the Former Day Saints or to the Latter Day Saints, so that they all have the authority to exercise faith in him and to expect by the exercise of their faith to enjoy the same blessings (¶26).

LECTURE FOURTH

Of Faith

1. Having shown in the third lecture that correct ideas of the character of God are necessary in order to the exercise of faith in him unto life and salvation, and that without correct ideas of his character, the minds of men could not have sufficient power with God to the exercise of faith necessary to the enjoyment of eternal life, and that correct ideas of his character lay a foundation, as far as his character is concerned, for the exercise of faith so as to enjoy the fullness of the blessing of the gospel of Jesus Christ, even that of Eternal glory, we shall now proceed to show the connection there is between correct ideas of the attributes of God and the exercise of faith in him unto eternal life.

2. Let us here observe that the real design which the God of Heaven had in view in making the human family acquainted with his attributes was that they, through the ideas of the existence of his attributes, might be enabled to exercise faith in him, and through the exercise of faith in him might obtain eternal life. For without the idea of the existence of the attributes which belong to God, the minds of men could not have power to exercise faith on him so as to lay hold upon eternal life. The God of Heaven, understanding most perfectly the constitution of human nature and the weakness of man, knew what was necessary to be revealed and what ideas must be planted in their minds in order that they might be enabled to exercise faith in him unto eternal life.

3. Having said so much, we shall proceed to examine the attributes of God as set forth in his revelations to the human family, and to show how necessary correct ideas of his attributes are to enable men to exercise faith in him. For without these ideas being planted in the minds of men, it would be out of the power of any person or persons to exercise faith in God so as to obtain eternal life. So that the divine communications made to man in the first instance were designed to establish in their minds the ideas necessary to enable them to exercise faith in God, and through this means to be partakers of his glory.

4. We have, in the revelations which he has given to the human family, the following account of his attributes:

5. First, knowledge. Acts 15:18 [Acts 9:8]: Known unto God are all his works from the beginning of the world. Isaiah 46:9,10 [Isa. 15:21]: Remember the former things of old, for I am God and there is none else; I am God, and there is none like me, declaring the end from the beginning and from ancient time the things that are not yet done, saying, My counsel shall stand and I will do all my pleasure.

6. Secondly, faith, or power. Hebrews 11:3 [Heb. 1:36]: Through faith we understand that the worlds were framed by the word of God. Genesis 1:1 [Gen. 2:2]: In the beginning God created the heaven and the earth. Isaiah 14:24,27 [Isa. 6:7]: The Lord of Hosts has sworn, saying, Surely as I have thought, so shall it come to pass, and as I have purposed, so shall it stand. For the Lord of Hosts has purposed, and who shall disannul it? And his hand is stretched out, and who shall turn it back?

7. Thirdly, justice. Psalms 89:14 [Ps. 89:3]: Justice and judgment are the habitation of thy throne. Isaiah 45:21 [Isa. 15:19]: Tell ye, and bring them near, yea, let them take counsel together: who has declared this from the ancient time? Have not I the Lord? And there is no God else beside me, a just God and a Savior. Zephaniah 3:5 [Zeph. 1:10]: The just Lord is in the midst thereof. Zechariah 9:9 [Zech. 1:26]: Rejoice greatly, O daughter of Zion, shout, O daughter of Jerusalem: behold, thy king comes unto thee; he is just and having salvation.

8. Fourthly, judgment. Psalms 89:14 [Ps. 89:3]: Justice and judgment are the habitation of thy throne. Deuteronomy 32:4 [Deut. 9:14]: He is the Rock, his work is perfect; for all his ways are judgment: a God of truth and without iniquity, just and right is he. Psalms 9:7 [Ps. 9:2]: But the Lord shall endure for ever: he has prepared his throne for judgment. Psalms 9:16 [Ps. 9:4]: The Lord is known by the judgment which he executes.

9. Fifthly, mercy. Psalms 89:15 [Ps. 89:3]: Mercy and truth shall go before his face. Exodus 34:6 [Ex. 18:6]: And the Lord passed by before him and proclaimed, The Lord, the Lord God, merciful and gracious. Nehemiah 9:17 [Neh. 2:36]: But thou art a God ready to pardon, gracious and merciful.

10. And sixthly, truth. Psalms 89:14 [Ps. 89:3]: Mercy and truth shall go before thy face. Exodus 34:6 [Ex. 18:6]: Long-suffering and abundant in goodness and truth. Deuteronomy 32:4 [Deut. 9:14]: He is the Rock, his work is perfect; for all his ways are judgment: a God of truth and without iniquity, just and right is he. Psalms 31:5 [Ps. 31:1]: Into thy hand I commit my spirit: thou hast redeemed me, O Lord God of truth.

11. By a little reflection it will be seen that the idea of the existence of these attributes in the Deity is necessary to enable any rational being to exercise faith in him. For without the idea of the existence of these attributes in the Deity men could not exercise faith in him for life and salvation, seeing that without the knowledge of all things, God would not be able to save any portion of his creatures. For it is by reason of the knowledge which he has of all things, from the beginning to the end, that enables him to give that understanding to his creatures, by which they are made partakers of eternal life; and if it were not for the idea existing in the minds of men that God had all knowledge, it would be impossible for them to exercise faith in him.

12. And it is not less necessary that men should have the idea of the existence of the attribute power in the Deity. For unless God had power over all things and was able, by his power, to control all things and thereby deliver his creatures who put their trust in him from the power of all beings that might seek their destruction, whether in Heaven, on earth, or in hell, men could not be saved. But with the idea of the existence of this attribute planted in the mind, men feel as though they had nothing to fear, who put their trust in God, believing that he has power to save all who come to him to the very uttermost.

13. It is also necessary, in order to the exercise of faith in God unto life and salvation, that men should have the idea of the existence of the attribute justice in him. For without the idea of the existence of the attribute justice in the Deity, men could not have confidence sufficiently to place themselves under his guidance and direction, for they would be filled with fear and doubt, lest the Judge of all the earth would not do right; and thus fear, or doubt, existing in the mind, would preclude the possibility of the exercise of faith in him for life and salvation. But when the idea of the existence of the attribute justice in the Deity is fairly planted in the mind, it leaves no room for doubt to get into the heart, and the mind is enabled to cast itself upon the Almighty without fear, and without doubt, and with most unshaken confidence, believing that the Judge of all the earth will do right.

14. It is also of equal importance that men should have the idea of the existence of the attribute judgment in God in order that they may exercise faith in him for life and salvation, for without the idea of the existence of this attribute in the Deity, it would be impossible for men to exercise faith in him for life and salvation, seeing that it is through the exercise of this attribute that the faithful in Christ Jesus are delivered out of the hands of those who seek their destruction. For if God were not to come out in swift judgment against the workers of iniquity and the powers of darkness, his saints could not be saved, for it is by judgment that the Lord delivers his saints out of the hands of all their enemies and those who reject the gospel of our Lord Jesus Christ. But no sooner is the idea of the existence of this attribute planted in the minds of men than it gives power to the mind for the exercise of faith and confidence in God and they are enabled, by faith, to lay hold on the promises which are set before them and wade through all the tribulations and afflictions to which they are subjected by reason of the persecution from those who know not God and obey not the gospel of our Lord Jesus Christ; believing that in due time the Lord will come out in swift judgment against their enemies, and they shall be cut off from before him, and that in his own due time he will bear them off conquerors and more than conquerors in all things.

15. And again, it is equally important that men should have the idea of the existence of the attribute mercy in the Deity in order to exercise faith in him for life and salvation. For without the idea of the existence of this attribute in the Deity, the spirits of the saints would faint in the midst of the tribulations, afflictions, and persecutions which they have to endure for righteousness' sake. But when the idea of the existence of this attribute is once established in the mind, it gives life and energy to the spirits of the saints, believing that the mercy of God will be poured out upon them in the midst of their afflictions, and that he will compassionate them in their sufferings, and that the mercy of God will lay hold of them and secure them in the arms of his love so that they will receive a full reward for all their sufferings.

16 And lastly, but not less important to the exercise of faith in God, is the idea of the existence of the attribute truth in him. For without the idea of the existence of this attribute the mind of man could have nothing upon which it could rest with certainty; all would be confusion and doubt. But with the idea of the existence of this attribute in the Deity in the mind, all the teachings, instructions, promises, and blessings become realities, and the mind is enabled to lay hold of them with certainty and confidence, believing that these things, and all that the Lord has said, shall be fulfilled in their time, and that all the cursings, denunciations, and judgments pronounced upon the heads of the unrighteous will also be executed in due time of the Lord. And by reason of the truth and veracity of him, the mind beholds its deliverance and salvation as being certain.

17. Let the mind once reflect sincerely and candidly upon the ideas of the existence of the before-mentioned attributes in the Deity and it will be seen that, as far as his attributes are concerned, there is a sure foundation laid for the exercise of faith in him for life and salvation. For inasmuch as God possesses the attribute knowledge, he can make all things known to his saints necessary for their salvation. And as he possesses the attribute power, he is able thereby to deliver them from the power of all enemies. And seeing also that justice is an attribute of the Deity, he will deal with them upon the principles of righteousness and equity, and a just reward

will be granted unto them for all their afflictions and sufferings for the truth's sake. And as judgment is an attribute of the Deity also, his saints can have the most unshaken confidence that they will, in due time, obtain a perfect deliverance out of the hands of all their enemies and a complete victory over all those who have sought their hurt and destruction. And as mercy is also an attribute of the Deity, his saints can have confidence that it will be exercised toward them, and through the exercise of that attribute toward them, comfort and consolation will be administered unto them abundantly amid all their afflictions and tribulations. And lastly, realizing that truth is an attribute of the Deity, the mind is led to rejoice amid all its trials and temptations, in hope of that glory which is to be brought at the revelation of Jesus Christ, and in view of that crown which is to be placed upon the heads of the saints in the day when the Lord shall distribute rewards unto them, and in prospect of that Eternal weight of glory which the Lord has promised to bestow upon them when he shall bring them into the midst of his throne to dwell in his presence eternally.

18. In view, then, of the existence of these attributes, the faith of the saints can become exceedingly strong, abounding in righteousness unto the praise and glory of God, and can exert its mighty influence in searching after wisdom and understanding until it has obtained a knowledge of all things that pertain to life and salvation.

19. Such, then, is the foundation which is laid through the revelation of the attributes of God for the exercise of faith in him for life and salvation, and seeing that these are attributes of the Deity, they are unchangeable—being the same yesterday, today, and for ever—which gives to the minds of the Latter Day Saints the same power and authority to exercise faith in God which the Former Day Saints had, so that all the saints, in this respect, have been, are, and will be alike until the end of time, for God never changes, therefore his attributes and character remain for ever the same. And as it is through the revelation of these that a foundation is laid for the exercise of faith in God unto life and salvation, the foundation, therefore, for the exercise of faith was, is, and ever will be the same, so that all men have had and will have an equal privilege.

Lecture Fourth

Questions and Answers on the Foregoing Principles

20. Question 1: What was shown in the third lecture?
Answer: It was shown that correct ideas of the character of God are necessary in order to exercise faith in him unto life and salvation, and that without correct ideas of his character, men could not have power to exercise faith in him unto life and salvation, but that correct ideas of his character, as far as his character is concerned in the exercise of faith in him, lay a sure foundation for the exercise of it (¶1).

21. Question 2: What object had the God of Heaven in revealing his attributes to men?
A: That through an acquaintance with his attributes they might be enabled to exercise faith in him so as to obtain eternal life (¶2).

22. Question 3: Could men exercise faith in God without an acquaintance with his attributes so as to be enabled to lay hold of eternal life?
A: They could not (¶¶2, 3).

23. Question 4: What account is given of the attributes of God in his revelations?
A: First, knowledge, secondly, faith, or power, thirdly, justice, fourthly, judgment, fifthly, mercy, and sixthly truth (¶¶4–10).

24. Question 5: Where are the revelations to be found which give this relation of the attributes of God?
A: In the Old and New Testaments, and they are quoted in the fourth lecture, fifth, sixth, seventh, eighth, ninth, and tenth paragraphs.*

25. Question 6: Is the idea of the existence of those attributes in the Deity necessary in order to enable any rational being to exercise faith in him unto life and salvation?
A: It is.

26. Question 7: How do you prove it?

A: By the eleventh, twelfth, thirteenth, fourteenth, fifteenth, and sixteenth paragraphs in this lecture.*

27. Question 8: Does the idea of the existence of these attributes in the Deity, as far as his attributes are concerned, enable a rational being to exercise faith in him unto life and salvation?
A: It does.

28. Question 9: How do you prove it?
A: By the seventeenth and eighteenth paragraphs.*

29. Question 10: Have the Latter Day Saints as much authority given them, through the revelation of the attributes of God, to exercise faith in him as the Former Day Saints had?
A: They have.

30. Question 11: How do you prove it?
A: By the nineteenth paragraph of this lecture.*

* Let the student turn and commit those paragraphs to memory.

LECTURE FIFTH

Of Faith

1. In our former lectures we treated of the being, character, perfections, and attributes of God. What we mean by perfections is: the perfections which belong to all the attributes of his nature. We shall, in this lecture, speak of the Godhead: we mean the Father, Son, and holy spirit.

2. There are two personages who constitute the great matchless, governing, and supreme power over all things—by whom all things were created and made, that are created and made, whether visible or invisible, whether in Heaven, on earth, or in the earth, under the earth, or throughout the immensity of space—they are the Father and the Son: the Father being a personage of spirit, glory, and power: possessing all perfection and fullness; the Son, who was in the bosom of the Father, a personage of tabernacle, made or fashioned like unto man, or being in the form and likeness of man, or rather, man was formed after his likeness and in his image—he is also the express image and likeness of the personage of the Father, possessing all the fullness of the Father, or the same fullness with the Father, being begotten of him, and was ordained from before the foundation of the world to be a propitiation for the sins of all those who should believe on his name, and is called the Son because of the flesh—and descended in suffering below that which man can suffer, or in other words, suffered greater sufferings and was exposed to more powerful contradictions than any man can be. But notwithstanding all this, he kept the law of God and remained without sin, showing thereby that it is in the power of man to keep the law and remain also without sin. And also, that by him a righteous judgment might come upon all flesh, and that all who walk not in the law of God may justly be condemned by the law and have no excuse for their sins. And he being the Only Begotten of the Father, full of grace and truth, and having overcome, received a fullness of the glory of the Father—possessing the same mind with the Father, which mind is the holy spirit that bears record of the Father and the Son, and these three are one, or in other words, these three constitute the great matchless, governing, and supreme power over all things, by whom all things were created and made

that were created and made. And these three constitute the Godhead and are one: the Father and the Son possessing the same mind, the same wisdom, glory, power, and fullness, filling all in all—the Son being filled with the fullness of the mind, glory, and power, or in other words, the spirit, glory, and power of the Father—possessing all knowledge and glory, and the same kingdom: sitting at the right hand of power, in the express image and likeness of the Father—a mediator for man—being filled with the fullness of the mind of the Father, or in other words, the spirit of the Father, which spirit is shed forth upon all who believe on his name and keep his commandments. And all those who keep his commandments shall grow up from grace to grace and become heirs of the Heavenly kingdom and joint-heirs with Jesus Christ, possessing the same mind, being transformed into the same image or likeness, even the express image of him who fills all in all: being filled with the fullness of his glory, and become one in him, even as the Father, Son, and holy spirit are one.

3. From the foregoing account of the Godhead which is given in his revelations, the saints have a sure foundation laid for the exercise of faith unto life and salvation through the atonement and mediation of Jesus Christ, by whose blood they have a forgiveness of sins and also a sure reward laid up for them in Heaven, even that of partaking of the fullness of the Father and the Son through the spirit. As the Son partakes of the fullness of the Father through the spirit, so the saints are, by the same spirit, to be partakers of the same fullness, to enjoy the same glory, for as the Father and the Son are one, so in like manner the saints are to be one in them: through the love of the Father, the mediation of Jesus Christ, and the gift of the holy spirit they are to be heirs of God and joint-heirs with Jesus Christ.

Questions and Answers on the Foregoing Principles

4. Question 1: Of what do the foregoing lectures treat?
Answer: Of the being, perfections, and attributes of the Deity (¶1).

5. Question 2: What are we to understand by the perfections of the Deity?

A: The perfections which belong to his attributes.

6. Question 3: How many personages are there in the Godhead?
A: Two: the Father and the Son (¶1).

7. Question 4: How do you prove that there are two personages in the Godhead?
A: By the Scriptures: Genesis 1:26 [Gen. 2:8]: And the Lord God said unto the Only Begotten, who was with him from the beginning, Let us make man in our image, after our likeness—and it was done. Genesis 3:22 [Gen. 2:19]: And the Lord God said unto the Only Begotten, Behold, the man is become as one of us: to know good and evil. John 17:5 [John 9:19]: And now, O Father, glorify thou me with thine own self with the glory which I had with thee before the world was (¶2)

8. Question 5: What is the Father?
A: He is a personage of glory and of power (¶2).

9. Question 6: How do you prove that the Father is a personage of glory and of power?
A: Isaiah 60:19 [Isa. 22:1]: The sun shall be no more thy light by day, neither for brightness shall the moon give light unto thee: but the Lord shall be unto thee an everlasting light, and thy God thy glory. 1 Chronicles 29:11 [1 Chr. 12:12]: Thine, O Lord, is the greatness, and the power, and the glory. Psalms 29:3 [Ps. 29:1]: The voice of the Lord is upon the waters: the God of glory thunders. Psalms 79:9 [Ps. 79:3]: Help us, O God of our salvation, for the glory of thy name. Romans 1:23 [Rom. 1:4]: And changed the glory of the incorruptible God into an image made like to corruptible men.

10. Secondly, of power. 1 Chronicles 29:11 [1 Chr. 12:12]: Thine, O Lord, is the greatness, and the power, and the glory. Jeremiah 32:17 [Jer. 13:3]: Ah! Lord God, behold, thou hast made the earth and the heavens by thy great power and stretched-out arm; and there is nothing too hard for thee. Deuteronomy 4:37 [Deut. 2:7]: And because he loved thy fathers, therefore he chose their seed after them and brought them out in his sight with his mighty power. 2 Samuel 22:33 [2 Sam. 10:9]: God is my strength and power. Job

26:7–14 [Job 10: 3–4]: He stretches out the north over the empty place, and hangs the earth upon nothing. He binds up the waters in his thick clouds and the cloud is not rent under them. He holds back the face of his throne and spreads his cloud upon it. He has compassed the waters with bounds until the day and night come to an end. The Pillars of Heaven tremble and are astonished at his reproof. He divides the sea with his power and by his understanding he smites through the proud. By his spirit he has garnished the heavens; his hand has formed the crooked serpent. Lo, these are parts of his ways, but how little a portion is heard of him? But the thunder of his power, who can understand?

11. Question 7: What is the Son?
A: First, He is a personage of tabernacle (¶2).

12. Question 8: How do you prove it?
A: John 14:9–11 [John 9:7]: Jesus says unto him, Have I been so long time with you and yet have you not known me, Philip? He that has seen me has seen the Father. And how do you say then, Show us the Father? Do you not believe that I am in the Father and the Father in me? The words that I speak unto you I speak not of myself, but the Father that dwells in me. He does the works. Believe me that I am in the Father and the Father in me.

13. Secondly, and being a personage of tabernacle was made or fashioned like unto man, or being in the form and likeness of man (¶2). Philippians 2:5–8 [Phil. 1:7]: Let this mind be in you which was also in Christ Jesus, who, being in the form of God, thought it not robbery to be equal with God, but made himself of no reputation, and took upon him the form of a servant, and was made in the likeness of man. And being found in fashion as a man, he humbled himself and became obedient unto death, even the death of the cross. Hebrews 2:14, 16 [Heb. 1:5]: Forasmuch then as the children are partakers of flesh and blood, he also himself likewise took part of the same. For verily he took not on him the nature of angels, but he took on him the seed of Abraham.

14. Thirdly, he is also in the likeness of the personage of the Father (¶2) Hebrews 1:1–3 [Heb. 1:1]: God, who at sundry times and in

divers manners spake in time past to the fathers by the prophets, has in these last days spoken unto us by his Son, whom he has appointed heir of all things, by whom also he made the worlds, who being the brightness of his glory and the express image of his person. Again, Philippians 2:5–6 [Phil. 1:7]: Let this mind be in you which was also in Christ Jesus, who, being in the form of God, thought it not robbery to be equal with God.

15. Question 9: Was it by the Father and the Son that all things were created and made that were created and made?
A: It was. Colossians 1:15–17 [Col. 1:3–4]: Who is the image of the invisible God, the firstborn of every creature, for by him were all things created that are in heaven, and that are in earth, visible and invisible, whether they be thrones, or dominions, principalities, or powers. All things were created by him and for him, and he is before all things, and by him all things consist. Genesis 1:1 [Gen. 2:2]: In the beginning God created the heavens and the earth. Hebrews 1:2 [Heb. 1:1]: God has in these last days spoken unto us by his Son, whom he has appointed heir of all things, by whom also he made the worlds.

16. Question 10: Does he possess the fullness of the Father?
A: He does. Colossians 1:19 [Col. 1:4]: For it pleased the Father that in him should all fullness dwell. Colossians 2:9 [Col. 1:7]: For in him dwells all the fullness of the Godhead bodily. Ephesians 1:23 [Eph. 1:3]: Which is his [Christ's] body, the fullness of him that fills all in all.

17. Question 11: Why was he called the Son?
A: Because of the flesh. Luke 1:35 [Luke 1:6]: That holy thing which shall be born of thee shall be called the Son of God. Matthew 3:16–17 [Matt. 2:4]: And Jesus, when he was baptized, went up straightway out of the water. And lo, the Heavens were opened unto him, and he (John) saw the spirit of God descending like a dove and lighting upon him, and lo, a voice from Heaven saying, This is my Beloved Son, in whom I am well pleased.

18. Question 12: Was he ordained of the Father, from before the foundation of the world, to be a propitiation for the sins of all those who should believe on his name?
A: He was. 1 Peter 1:18–20 [1 Pet. 1:4]: For as much as you know that you were not redeemed with corruptible things, as silver and gold, from your vain conversation (received by tradition from your fathers), but with the precious blood of Christ, as of a lamb without blemish and without spot, who verily was foreordained before the foundation of the world, but was manifested in these last times for you. Revelation 13:8 [Rev. 4:8]: And all that dwell upon the earth shall worship him [the beast] whose names are not written in the book of life of the Lamb slain from the foundation of the world. 1 Corinthians 2:7 [1 Cor. 1:7]: But we speak the wisdom of God in a mystery, even the hidden mystery which God ordained before the world unto our glory.

19. Question 13: Do the Father and the Son possess the same mind?
A: They do. John 5:30 [John 5:5]: I (Christ) can of my own self do nothing. As I hear, I judge, and my judgment is just, because I seek not my own will, but the will of the Father who sent me. John 6:38 [John 5:14]: For I (Christ) came down from Heaven not to do my own will, but the will of him that sent me. John 10:30 [John 6:29]: I (Christ) and my Father are one.

20. Question 14: What is this mind?
A: The holy spirit. John 15:26 [John 9:13]: But when the Comforter is come, whom I will send unto you from the Father, even the spirit of truth which proceeds from the Father, he shall testify of me (Christ). Galatians 4:6 [Gal. 1:13]: And because you are sons, God has sent forth the spirit of his Son into your hearts.

21. Question 15: Do the Father, Son, and holy spirit constitute the Godhead?
A: They do (¶2) Let the student commit this paragraph to memory.

22. Question 16: Does the believer in Christ Jesus, through the gift of the spirit, become one with the Father and the Son, as the Father and the Son are one?

A: They do. John 17:20–21 [John 9:21]: Neither pray I for these [the apostles] alone, but for them also who shall believe on me through their word, that they all may be one as thou, Father, art in me, and I in thee, that they also may be one in us, that the world may believe that thou hast sent me.

23. Question 17: Does the foregoing account of the Godhead lay a sure foundation for the exercise of faith in him unto life and salvation?
A: It does.

24. Question 18: How do you prove it?
A: By the third paragraph of this lecture.

Let the student commit this also.

LECTURE SIXTH

Of Faith

1. Having treated, in the preceding lectures, of the ideas of the character, perfections, and attributes of God, we next proceed to treat of the knowledge which persons must have that the course of life which they pursue is according to the will of God, in order that they may be enabled to exercise faith in him unto life and salvation.

2. This knowledge supplies an important place in revealed religion, for it was by reason of it that the ancients were enabled to endure as seeing him who is invisible. An actual knowledge to any person that the course of life which he pursues is according to the will of God is essentially necessary to enable him to have that confidence in God, without which no person can obtain eternal life. It was this that enabled the ancient saints to endure all their afflictions and persecutions and to take joyfully the spoiling of their goods, knowing (not believing merely) that they had a more enduring substance (Hebrews 10:34) [Heb. 1:34].

3. Having the assurance that they were pursuing a course which was agreeable to the will of God, they were enabled to take not only the spoiling of their goods and the wasting of their substance joyfully, but also to suffer death in its most horrid forms, knowing (not merely believing) that when this earthly house of their tabernacle was dissolved, they had a building of God, a house not made with hands, eternal in the Heavens (2 Corinthians 5:1) [2 Cor. 1:15].

4. Such was and always will be the situation of the saints of God: that unless they have an actual knowledge that the course that they are pursuing is according to the will of God, they will grow weary in their minds and faint, for such has been and always will be the opposition in the hearts of unbelievers and those that know not God, against the pure and unadulterated religion of Heaven (the only thing which ensures eternal life), that they will persecute to the uttermost all that worship God according to his revelations, receive the truth in the love of it, and submit themselves to be guided and directed by his will, and drive them to such extremities

that nothing short of an actual knowledge of their being the favorites of Heaven, and of their having embraced that order of things which God has established for the redemption of man, will enable them to exercise that confidence in him necessary for them to overcome the world and obtain that crown of glory which is laid up for them that fear God.

5. For a man to lay down his all, his character and reputation, his honor and applause, his good name among men, his houses, his lands, his brothers and sisters, his wife and children, and even his own life also, counting all things but filth and dross for the excellency of the knowledge of Jesus Christ, requires more than mere belief, or supposition that he is doing the will of God, but actual knowledge, realizing that when these sufferings are ended he will enter into Eternal rest and be a partaker of the glory of God.

6. For unless a person does know that he is walking according to the will of God, it would be offering an insult to the dignity of the Creator were he to say that he would be a partaker of his glory when he should be done with the things of this life. But when he has this knowledge, and most assuredly knows that he is doing the will of God, his confidence can be equally strong that he will be a partaker of the glory of God.

7. Let us here observe that a religion that does not require the sacrifice of all things never has power sufficient to produce the faith necessary unto life and salvation. For from the first existence of man, the faith necessary unto the enjoyment of life and salvation never could be obtained without the sacrifice of all earthly things: it was through this sacrifice, and this only, that God has ordained that men should enjoy eternal life, and it is through the medium of the sacrifice of all earthly things that men do actually know that they are doing the things that are well pleasing in the sight of God. When a man has offered in sacrifice all that he has for the truth's sake, not even withholding his life, and believing before God that he has been called to make this sacrifice because he seeks to do his will, he does know most assuredly that God does and will accept his sacrifice and offering, and that he has not nor will not seek his face in vain.

Lecture Sixth

Under these circumstances, then, he can obtain the faith necessary for him to lay hold on eternal life.

8. It is in vain for persons to fancy to themselves that they are heirs with those, or can be heirs with them, who have offered their all in sacrifice, and by this means obtained faith in God and favor with him so as to obtain eternal life, unless they in like manner offer unto him the same sacrifice, and through that offering obtain the knowledge that they are accepted of him.

9. It was in offering sacrifices that Abel, the first martyr, obtained knowledge that he was accepted of God. And from the days of righteous Abel to the present time, the knowledge that men have that they are accepted in the sight of God is obtained by offering sacrifice. And in the last days, before the Lord comes, he is to gather together his saints who have made a covenant with him by sacrifice. Psalms 50:3–5 [Ps. 50:1]: Our God shall come and shall not keep silence. A fire shall devour before him and it shall be very tempestuous round about him. He shall call to the heavens from above and to the earth that he may judge his people. Gather my saints together unto me, those that have made a covenant unto me by sacrifice.

10. Those, then, who make the sacrifice will have the testimony that their course is pleasing in the sight of God, and those who have this testimony will have faith to lay hold on eternal life and will be enabled, through faith, to endure unto the end and receive the crown that is laid up for them that love the appearing of our Lord Jesus Christ. But those who do not make the sacrifice cannot enjoy this faith because men are dependent upon this sacrifice in order to obtain this faith, therefore they cannot lay hold upon eternal life because the revelations of God do not guarantee unto them the authority so to do, and without this guarantee faith could not exist.

11. All the saints of whom we have account in all the revelations of God which are extant obtained the knowledge which they had of their acceptance in his sight through the sacrifice which they offered unto him, and through the knowledge thus obtained, their faith became sufficiently strong to lay hold upon the promise of

eternal life, and to endure as seeing him who is invisible, and were enabled through faith to combat the powers of darkness, contend against the wiles of the adversary, overcome the world, and obtain the end of their faith, even the salvation of their souls.

12. But those who have not made this sacrifice to God do not know that the course which they pursue is well-pleasing in his sight, for whatever may be their belief or their opinion, it is a matter of doubt and uncertainty in their mind, and where doubt and uncertainty is, there faith is not, nor can it be. For doubt and faith do not exist in the same person at the same time. So that persons whose minds are under doubts and fears cannot have unshaken confidence, and where unshaken confidence is not, there faith is weak, and where faith is weak, the persons will not be able to contend against all the opposition, tribulations, and afflictions which they will have to encounter in order to be heirs of God and joint-heirs with Christ Jesus, and they will grow weary in their minds, and the adversary will have power over them and destroy them.

13. This lecture is so plain, and the facts set forth so self-evident, that it is deemed unnecessary to form a catechism upon it. The student is therefore instructed to commit the whole to memory.

LECTURE SEVENTH

Of Faith

1. In the preceding lectures we treated of what faith was and of the object on which it rested; agreeably to our plan we now proceed to speak of its effects:

2. As we have seen in our former lectures, that faith was the principle of action and of power in all intelligent beings, both in Heaven and on earth, it will not be expected that we will, in a lecture of this description, attempt to unfold all its effects; neither is it necessary to our purpose so to do, for it would embrace all things in Heaven and on earth, and encompass all the creations of God with all their endless varieties. For no world has yet been framed that was not framed by faith, neither has there been an intelligent being on any of God's creations who did not get there by reason of faith as it existed in himself or in some other being, nor has there been a change or a revolution in any of the creations of God but it has been effected by faith. Neither will there be a change or a revolution unless it is effected in the same way in any of the vast creations of the Almighty, for it is by faith that the Deity works.

3. Let us here offer some explanation in relation to faith that our meaning may be clearly comprehended. We ask, then: What are we to understand by a man's working by faith? We answer: We understand that when a man works by faith, he works by mental exertion instead of physical force; it is by words, instead of exerting his physical powers with which every being works, when he works by faith—God said, Let there be light, and there was light—Joshua spake and the great lights which God had created stood still—Elijah commanded and the heavens were stayed for the space of three years and six months so that it did not rain; he again commanded and the heavens gave forth rain—all this was done by faith; and the Savior says, If you have faith as a grain of mustard seed, say to this mountain, Remove—and it will remove, or say to that sycamine tree, Be ye plucked up and planted in the midst of the sea—and it shall obey you. Faith, then, works by words, and with these its mightiest works have been and will be performed.

4. It surely will not be required of us to prove that this is the principle upon which all eternity has acted and will act, for every reflecting mind must know that it is by reason of this power that all the hosts of Heaven perform their works of wonder, majesty, and glory: Angels move from place to place by virtue of this power—it is by reason of it that they are enabled to descend from Heaven to earth. And were it not for the power of faith, they never could be ministering spirits to them who should be heirs of salvation, neither could they act as Heavenly messengers, for they would be destitute of the power necessary to enable them to do the will of God.

5. It is only necessary for us to say that the whole visible creation, as it now exists, is the effect of faith—it was faith by which it was framed, and it is by the power of faith that it continues in its organized form, and by which the planets move round their orbits and sparkle forth their glory. So then faith is truly the first principle in the science of theology, and when understood, leads the mind back to the beginning and carries it forward to the end, or in other words, from eternity to eternity.

6. As faith, then, is the principle by which the Heavenly hosts perform their works and by which they enjoy all their felicity, we might expect to find it set forth in a revelation from God as the principle upon which his creatures here below must act in order to obtain the felicities enjoyed by the saints in the Eternal world, and that when God would undertake to raise up men for the enjoyment of himself, he would teach them the necessity of living by faith and the impossibility there was of their enjoying the blessedness of eternity without it, seeing that all the blessings of eternity are the effects of faith.

7. Therefore, it is said, and appropriately too, that without faith it is impossible to please God. If it should be asked, Why is it impossible to please God without faith?—the answer would be, Because without faith it is impossible for men to be saved. And as God desires the salvation of man, he must of course desire that they should have faith, and he could not be pleased unless they had, or else he could be pleased with their destruction.

8. From this we learn that the many exhortations, which have been given by inspired men to those who had received the word of the Lord to have faith in him, were not mere commonplace matters, but were for the best of all reasons, and that was because without it there was no salvation—neither in this world nor in that which is to come. When men begin to live by faith they begin to draw near to God. And when faith is perfected, they are like him; and because he is saved, they are saved also, for they will be in the same situation he is in because they have come to him; and when he appears, they shall be like him, for they will see him as he is.

9. As all the visible creation is an effect of faith, so is salvation also (we mean salvation in its most extensive latitude of interpretation, whether it is temporal or spiritual). In order to have this subject clearly set before the mind, let us ask: What situation must a person be in in order to be saved? Or what is the difference between a saved man and one who is not saved? We answer from what we have before seen of the Heavenly worlds: They must be persons who can work by faith and who are able, by faith, to be ministering spirits to them who shall be heirs of salvation. And they must have faith to enable them to act in the presence of the Lord, otherwise they cannot be saved. And what constitutes the real difference between a saved person and one not saved is the difference in the degree of their faith—one's faith has become perfect enough to lay hold upon eternal life and the other's has not. But to be a little more particular, let us ask: Where shall we find a prototype into whose likeness we may be assimilated, in order that we may be made partakers of life and salvation? Or in other words, where shall we find a saved being? For if we can find a saved being, we may ascertain without much difficulty what all others must be in order to be saved—they must be like that individual or they cannot be saved. We think that it will not be a matter of dispute that two beings who are unlike each other cannot both be saved, for whatever constitutes the salvation of one will constitute the salvation of every creature which will be saved. And if we find one saved being in all existence, we may see what all others must be or else not be saved. We ask, then: Where is the prototype? Or where is the saved being? We conclude as to the answer of this question there will be no dispute among those who believe the Bible that it is Christ. All will agree in this, that he is the

prototype or standard of salvation, or in other words, that he is a saved being. And if we should continue our interrogation, and ask how it is that he is saved, the answer would be, because he is a just and holy being. And if he were anything different from what he is he would not be saved, for his salvation depends on his being precisely what he is and nothing else. For if it were possible for him to change in the least degree, so sure he would fail of salvation and lose all his dominion, power, authority, and glory, which constitutes salvation. For salvation consists in the glory, authority, majesty, power, and dominion which Jehovah possesses, and in nothing else, and no being can possess it but himself or one like him. Thus says John in his first epistle, 3:2,3 [1 John 1:13]: Behold, now we are the sons of God, and it doth not appear what we shall be; but we know that when he shall appear we shall be like him, for we shall see him as he is. And any man that has this hope in him purifies himself, even as he is pure. Why purify himself as he is pure? Because if they do not, they cannot be like him.

10. The Lord said unto Moses, Leviticus 19:2 [Lev. 9:1]: Speak unto all the congregation of the children of Israel and say unto them, Ye shall be holy, for I the Lord your God am holy. And Peter says, first epistle, 1:15,16 [1 Pet. 1:3]: But as he who has called you is holy, so be ye holy in all manner of conversation, because it is written: Be ye holy, for I am holy. And the Savior says, Matthew 5:48 [Matt. 3:26]: Be ye perfect, even as your Father who is in Heaven is perfect. If any should ask, Why all these sayings?—the answer is to be found from what is before quoted from John's epistle, that when he (the Lord) shall appear, the saints will be like him, and if they are not holy as he is holy, and perfect as he is perfect, they cannot be like him, for no being can enjoy his glory without possessing his perfections and holiness, no more than they could reign in his kingdom without his power.

11. This clearly sets forth the propriety of the Savior's saying, recorded in John's testimony, 14:12 [John 9:7]: Verily, verily I say unto you, he that believeth on me, the works that I do shall he do also, and greater works than these, because I go unto the Father. This, taken in connection with some of the sayings in the Savior's prayer, recorded in the 17th chapter, gives great clearness to his

Lecture Seventh

expressions. He says, in the 20–24 [John 9:21]: Neither pray I for these alone, but for them also who shall believe on me through their words, that they all may be one as thou, Father, art in me and I in thee, that they also may be one in us, that the world may believe that thou hast sent me. And the glory which thou gavest me I have given them, that they may be one even as we are one—I in them and thou in me—that they may be made perfect in one, and that the world may know that thou hast sent me, and hast loved them as thou hast loved me. Father, I will that they also, whom thou hast given me, be with me where I am, that they may behold my glory which thou hast given me, for thou lovedst me before the foundation of the world.

12. All these sayings, put together, give as clear an account of the state of the glorified saints as language could give—the works that Jesus did they were to do, and greater works than those which he did among them should they do, and that because he went to the Father. He does not say that they should do these works in time, but they should do greater works because he went to the Father. He says, in the 24th verse [John 9:21]: Father, I will that they also, whom thou hast given me, be with me where I am, that they may behold my glory. These sayings, taken in connection, make it very plain that the greater works which those that believed on his name were to do were to be done in eternity where he is going and where they should behold his glory. He had said in another part of his prayer that he desired of his Father that those who believed on him should be one in him, as he and the Father were one in each other: Neither pray I for these (the apostles) alone, but for them also who shall believe on me through their words, that they all may be one. That is, they who believe on him through the apostles' words, as well as the apostles themselves: that they all may be one, as thou, Father, art in me and I in thee, that they also may be one in us.

13. What language can be plainer than this? The Savior surely intended to be understood by his disciples, and he so spake that they might understand him. For he declares to his Father in language not to be easily mistaken that he wanted his disciples, even all of them, to be as himself and the Father: for as he and the Father were one, so they might be one with them. And what is said

in the 22nd verse [John 9:20] is calculated to more firmly establish this belief, if it needs anything to establish it. He says, And the glory which thou gavest me, I have given them, that they may be one even as we are one. As much as to say that unless they have the glory which the Father had given him, they could not be one with them, for he says he had given them the glory that the Father had given him, that they might be one, or in other words, to make them one.

14. This fills up the measure of information on this subject and shows most clearly that the Savior wished his disciples to understand that they were to be partakers with him in all things, not even his glory excepted.

15. It is scarcely necessary here to observe what we have previously noticed, that the glory which the Father and the Son have is because they are just and holy beings, and that if they were lacking in one attribute or perfection which they have, the glory which they have never could be enjoyed by them, for it requires them to be precisely what they are in order to enjoy it. And if the Savior gives this glory to any others, he must do it in the very way set forth in his prayer to his Father: by making them one with him as he and the Father are one. In so doing he would give them the glory which the Father has given him; and when his disciples are made one with the Father and the Son, as the Father and the Son are one, who cannot see the propriety of the Savior's saying, The works which I do shall they do, and greater works than these shall they do, because I go to the Father?

16. These teachings of the Savior most clearly show unto us the nature of salvation, and what he proposed unto the human family when he proposed to save them: that he proposed to make them like unto himself, and he was like the Father, the great prototype of all saved beings. And for any portion of the human family to be assimilated into their likeness is to be saved, and to be unlike them is to be destroyed. And on this hinge turns the door of salvation.

17. Who cannot see, then, that salvation is the effect of faith? For as we have previously observed, all the Heavenly beings work by this principle, and it is because they are able so to do that they are saved,

for nothing but this could save them. And this is the lesson which the God of Heaven, by the mouth of all his holy prophets, has been endeavoring to teach to the world. Hence we are told that without faith it is impossible to please God, and that the salvation is of faith, that it might be by grace, to the end the promise might be sure to all the seed (Romans 4:16) [Rom. 1:20]—And that Israel, who followed after the law of righteousness, has not attained to the law of righteousness. Wherefore? Because they sought it not by faith, but as it were by the works of the law, for they stumbled at that stumbling stone (Romans 9:32) [Rom. 1:45]. And Jesus said unto the man who brought his son to him to get the devil who tormented him cast out, If thou canst believe, all things are possible to him that believeth (Mark 9:23) [Mark 5:9]. These, with a multitude of other scriptures which might be quoted, plainly set forth the light in which the Savior, as well as the Former Day Saints, viewed the plan of salvation, that it was a system of faith—it begins with faith and continues by faith. And every blessing which is obtained in relation to it is the effect of faith, whether it pertains to this life or that which is to come. To this all the revelations of God bear witness. If there were children of promise, they were the effects of faith, not even the Savior of the world excepted: Blessed is she that believed, said Elizabeth to Mary when she went to visit her, for there shall be a performance of the things which were told her of the Lord (Luke 1:45) [Luke 1:7]. Nor was the birth of John the Baptist the less a matter of faith, for in order that his father Zacharias might believe he was struck dumb. And through the whole history of the scheme of life and salvation, it is a matter of faith: every man received according to his faith—according as his faith was, so were his blessings and privileges, and nothing was withheld from him when his faith was sufficient to receive it. He could stop the mouths of lions, quench the violence of fire, escape the edge of the sword, wax valiant in fight, and put to flight the armies of the aliens; women could, by their faith, receive the dead children to life again—in a word, there was nothing impossible with them who had faith. All things were in subjection to the Former Day Saints according as their faith was—by their faith they could obtain Heavenly visions, the ministering of angels, have knowledge of the spirits of just men made perfect, of the general assembly and church of the Firstborn (whose names are written in Heaven), of God, the judge of all, of

Jesus, the Mediator of the new covenant, and become familiar with the third Heavens, see and hear things which were not only unutterable, but were unlawful to utter. Peter, in view of the power of faith, 2nd epistle, 1:2–3 [2 Pet. 1:1] says to the Former Day Saints, Grace and peace be multiplied unto you through the knowledge of God and of Jesus our Lord, according as his divine power hath given unto us all things that pertain unto life and godliness, through the knowledge of him that has called us unto glory and virtue. In the first epistle, 1:3–5 [1 Pet. 1:2] he says, Blessed be the God and Father of our Lord Jesus Christ, who according to his abundant mercy has begotten us again unto a lively hope by the resurrection of Jesus Christ from the dead to an inheritance incorruptible, and undefiled, and that fadeth not away, reserved in Heaven for you who are kept by the power of God through faith unto salvation, ready to be revealed in the last time.

18. These sayings, put together, show the Apostle's views most clearly, so as to admit of no mistake on the mind of any individual. He says that all things that pertain to life and godliness were given unto them through the knowledge of God and our Savior Jesus Christ. And if the question is asked: How were they to obtain the knowledge of God? (for there is a great difference between believing in God and knowing him—knowledge implies more than faith; and notice that all things that pertain to life and godliness were given through knowledge of God)—the answer is given: Through faith they were to obtain this knowledge; and having power by faith to obtain the knowledge of God, they could with it obtain all other things which pertain to life and godliness.

19. By these sayings of the Apostle we learn that it was by obtaining a knowledge of God that men got all things which pertain to life and godliness, and this knowledge was the effect of faith. So that all things which pertain to life and godliness are the effects of faith.

20. From this we may extend as far as any circumstances may require, whether on earth or in Heaven, and we will find it the testimony of all inspired men or Heavenly messengers that all things that pertain to life and godliness are the effects of faith and nothing else: all learning, wisdom, and prudence fail, and

everything else as a means of salvation but faith. This is the reason that the fishermen of Galilee could teach the world—because they sought by faith and by faith obtained. And this is the reason that Paul counted all things but filth and dross—what he formerly called his gain he called his loss; yea, and he counted all things but loss for the excellency of the knowledge of Christ Jesus the Lord (Philippians 3:7-10) [Phil. 1:12]. Because, to obtain the faith by which he could enjoy the knowledge of Christ Jesus the Lord, he had to suffer the loss of all things. This is the reason that the Former Day Saints knew more and understood more of Heaven and of Heavenly things than all others beside, because this information is the effect of faith—to be obtained by no other means. And this is the reason that men, as soon as they lose their faith, run into strifes, contentions, darkness, and difficulties. For the knowledge which tends to life disappears with faith, but returns when faith returns, for when faith comes, it brings its train of attendants with it—apostles, prophets, evangelists, pastors, teachers, gifts, wisdom, knowledge, miracles, healings, tongues, interpretation of tongues, etc. All these appear when faith appears on the earth and disappear when it disappears from the earth. For these are the effects of faith, and always have and always will attend it. For where faith is, there will the knowledge of God be also, with all things which pertain thereto—revelations, visions, and dreams, as well as every other necessary thing, in order that the possessors of faith may be perfected and obtain salvation. For God must change, otherwise faith will prevail with him. And he who possesses it will, through it, obtain all necessary knowledge and wisdom until he shall know God and the Lord Jesus Christ whom he has sent, whom to know is eternal life. Amen.

Appendix: Chronology of the Fathers

www.ingramcontent.com/pod-product-compliance
Lightning Source LLC
Chambersburg PA
CBHW060045230426
43661CB00004B/658